Life Application Bible Studies
1 & 2 THESSALONIANS / PHILEMON

APPLICATION® BIBLE STUDIES

Part 1:
Complete text of 1 & 2 Thessalonians / Philemon with study notes and features from the *Life Application Study Bible*

Part 2:
Thirteen lessons for individual or group study

Study questions written and edited by

Wightman Weese
Rev. David R. Veerman
Dr. James C. Galvin
Dr. Bruce B. Barton
Daryl J. Lucas

New Living
Translation®

Tyndale House Publishers, Inc.
Carol Stream, Illinois

Visit Tyndale's exciting Web sites at www.newlivingtranslation.com and www.tyndale.com.

New Living Translation, NLT, the New Living Translation logo, and Life Application are registered trademarks of Tyndale House Publishers, Inc.

Life Application Bible Studies: 1 & 2 Thessalonians / Philemon

ISBN 978-1-4143-2653-5

Printed in the United States of America

15   14   13   12   11   10
6   5   4   3   2   1

CONTENTS

A NOTE TO READERS

The *Holy Bible,* New Living Translation, was first published in 1996. It quickly became one of the most popular Bible translations in the English-speaking world. While the NLT's influence was rapidly growing, the Bible Translation Committee determined that an additional investment in scholarly review and text refinement could make it even better. So shortly after its initial publication, the committee began an eight-year process with the purpose of increasing the level of the NLT's precision without sacrificing its easy-to-understand quality. This second-generation text was completed in 2004 and is reflected in this edition of the New Living Translation. An additional update with minor changes was subsequently introduced in 2007.

The goal of any Bible translation is to convey the meaning and content of the ancient Hebrew, Aramaic, and Greek texts as accurately as possible to contemporary readers. The challenge for our translators was to create a text that would communicate as clearly and powerfully to today's readers as the original texts did to readers and listeners in the ancient biblical world. The resulting translation is easy to read and understand, while also accurately communicating the meaning and content of the original biblical texts. The NLT is a general-purpose text especially good for study, devotional reading, and reading aloud in worship services.

We believe that the New Living Translation—which combines the latest biblical scholarship with a clear, dynamic writing style—will communicate God's word powerfully to all who read it. We publish it with the prayer that God will use it to speak his timeless truth to the church and the world in a fresh, new way.

The Publishers
October 2007

INTRODUCTION TO THE
NEW LIVING TRANSLATION

Translation Philosophy and Methodology

English Bible translations tend to be governed by one of two general translation theories. The first theory has been called "formal-equivalence," "literal," or "word-for-word" translation. According to this theory, the translator attempts to render each word of the original language into English and seeks to preserve the original syntax and sentence structure as much as possible in translation. The second theory has been called "dynamic-equivalence," "functional-equivalence," or "thought-for-thought" translation. The goal of this translation theory is to produce in English the closest natural equivalent of the message expressed by the original-language text, both in meaning and in style.

Both of these translation theories have their strengths. A formal-equivalence translation preserves aspects of the original text—including ancient idioms, term consistency, and original-language syntax—that are valuable for scholars and professional study. It allows a reader to trace formal elements of the original-language text through the English translation. A dynamic-equivalence translation, on the other hand, focuses on translating the message of the original-language text. It ensures that the meaning of the text is readily apparent to the contemporary reader. This allows the message to come through with immediacy, without requiring the reader to struggle with foreign idioms and awkward syntax. It also facilitates serious study of the text's message and clarity in both devotional and public reading.

The pure application of either of these translation philosophies would create translations at opposite ends of the translation spectrum. But in reality, all translations contain a mixture of these two philosophies. A purely formal-equivalence translation would be unintelligible in English, and a purely dynamic-equivalence translation would risk being unfaithful to the original. That is why translations shaped by dynamic-equivalence theory are usually quite literal when the original text is relatively clear, and the translations shaped by formal-equivalence theory are sometimes quite dynamic when the original text is obscure.

The translators of the New Living Translation set out to render the message of the original texts of Scripture into clear, contemporary English. As they did so, they kept the concerns of both formal-equivalence and dynamic-equivalence in mind. On the one hand, they translated as simply and literally as possible when that approach yielded an accurate, clear, and natural English text. Many words and phrases were rendered literally and consistently into English, preserving essential literary and rhetorical devices, ancient metaphors, and word choices that give structure to the text and provide echoes of meaning from one passage to the next.

On the other hand, the translators rendered the message more dynamically when the literal rendering was hard to understand, was misleading, or yielded archaic or foreign wording. They clarified difficult metaphors and terms to aid in the reader's understanding. The translators first struggled with the meaning of the words and phrases in the ancient context; then they rendered the message into clear, natural English. Their goal was to be both faithful to the ancient texts and eminently readable. The result is a translation that is both exegetically accurate and idiomatically powerful.

Translation Process and Team

To produce an accurate translation of the Bible into contemporary English, the translation team needed the skills necessary to enter into the thought patterns of the ancient authors and then to render their ideas, connotations, and effects into clear, contemporary English.

To begin this process, qualified biblical scholars were needed to interpret the meaning of the original text and to check it against our base English translation. In order to guard against personal and theological biases, the scholars needed to represent a diverse group of evangelicals who would employ the best exegetical tools. Then to work alongside the scholars, skilled English stylists were needed to shape the text into clear, contemporary English.

With these concerns in mind, the Bible Translation Committee recruited teams of scholars that represented a broad spectrum of denominations, theological perspectives, and backgrounds within the worldwide evangelical community. Each book of the Bible was assigned to three different scholars with proven expertise in the book or group of books to be reviewed. Each of these scholars made a thorough review of a base translation and submitted suggested revisions to the appropriate Senior Translator. The Senior Translator then reviewed and summarized these suggestions and proposed a first-draft revision of the base text. This draft served as the basis for several additional phases of exegetical and stylistic committee review. Then the Bible Translation Committee jointly reviewed and approved every verse of the final translation.

Throughout the translation and editing process, the Senior Translators and their scholar teams were given a chance to review the editing done by the team of stylists. This ensured that exegetical errors would not be introduced late in the process and that the entire Bible Translation Committee was happy with the final result. By choosing a team of qualified scholars and skilled stylists and by setting up a process that allowed their interaction throughout the process, the New Living Translation has been refined to preserve the essential formal elements of the original biblical texts, while also creating a clear, understandable English text.

The New Living Translation was first published in 1996. Shortly after its initial publication, the Bible Translation Committee began a process of further committee review and translation refinement. The purpose of this continued revision was to increase the level of precision without sacrificing the text's easy-to-understand quality. This second-edition text was completed in 2004, and an additional update with minor changes was subsequently introduced in 2007. This printing of the New Living Translation reflects the updated 2007 text.

Written to Be Read Aloud
It is evident in Scripture that the biblical documents were written to be read aloud, often in public worship (see Nehemiah 8; Luke 4:16-20; 1 Timothy 4:13; Revelation 1:3). It is still the case today that more people will hear the Bible read aloud in church than are likely to read it for themselves. Therefore, a new translation must communicate with clarity and power when it is read publicly. Clarity was a primary goal for the NLT translators, not only to facilitate private reading and understanding, but also to ensure that it would be excellent for public reading and make an immediate and powerful impact on any listener.

The Texts behind the New Living Translation
The Old Testament translators used the Masoretic Text of the Hebrew Bible as represented in *Biblia Hebraica Stuttgartensia* (1977), with its extensive system of textual notes; this is an update of Rudolf Kittel's *Biblia Hebraica* (Stuttgart, 1937). The translators also further compared the Dead Sea Scrolls, the Septuagint and other Greek manuscripts, the Samaritan Pentateuch, the Syriac Peshitta, the Latin Vulgate, and any other versions or manuscripts that shed light on the meaning of difficult passages.

The New Testament translators used the two standard editions of the Greek New Testament: the *Greek New Testament*, published by the United Bible Societies (UBS, fourth revised edition, 1993), and *Novum Testamentum Graece*, edited by Nestle and Aland (NA, twenty-seventh edition, 1993). These two editions, which have the same text but differ in punctuation and textual notes, represent, for the most part, the best in modern textual scholarship. However, in cases where strong textual or other scholarly evidence supported the decision, the translators sometimes chose to differ from the UBS and NA Greek texts and followed variant readings found in other ancient witnesses. Significant textual variants of this sort are always noted in the textual notes of the New Living Translation.

Translation Issues
The translators have made a conscious effort to provide a text that can be easily understood by the typical reader of modern English. To this end, we sought to use only vocabulary and

language structures in common use today. We avoided using language likely to become quickly dated or that reflects only a narrow subdialect of English, with the goal of making the New Living Translation as broadly useful and timeless as possible.

But our concern for readability goes beyond the concerns of vocabulary and sentence structure. We are also concerned about historical and cultural barriers to understanding the Bible, and we have sought to translate terms shrouded in history and culture in ways that can be immediately understood. To this end:

- We have converted ancient weights and measures (for example, "ephah" [a unit of dry volume] or "cubit" [a unit of length]) to modern English (American) equivalents, since the ancient measures are not generally meaningful to today's readers. Then in the textual footnotes we offer the literal Hebrew, Aramaic, or Greek measures, along with modern metric equivalents.

- Instead of translating ancient currency values literally, we have expressed them in common terms that communicate the message. For example, in the Old Testament, "ten shekels of silver" becomes "ten pieces of silver" to convey the intended message. In the New Testament, we have often translated the "denarius" as "the normal daily wage" to facilitate understanding. Then a footnote offers: "Greek *a denarius,* the payment for a full day's wage." In general, we give a clear English rendering and then state the literal Hebrew, Aramaic, or Greek in a textual footnote.

- Since the names of Hebrew months are unknown to most contemporary readers, and since the Hebrew lunar calendar fluctuates from year to year in relation to the solar calendar used today, we have looked for clear ways to communicate the time of year the Hebrew months (such as Abib) refer to. When an expanded or interpretive rendering is given in the text, a textual note gives the literal rendering. Where it is possible to define a specific ancient date in terms of our modern calendar, we use modern dates in the text. A textual footnote then gives the literal Hebrew date and states the rationale for our rendering. For example, Ezra 6:15 pinpoints the date when the postexilic Temple was completed in Jerusalem: "the third day of the month Adar." This was during the sixth year of King Darius's reign (that is, 515 B.C.). We have translated that date as March 12, with a footnote giving the Hebrew and identifying the year as 515 B.C.

- Since ancient references to the time of day differ from our modern methods of denoting time, we have used renderings that are instantly understandable to the modern reader. Accordingly, we have rendered specific times of day by using approximate equivalents in terms of our common "o'clock" system. On occasion, translations such as "at dawn the next morning" or "as the sun was setting" have been used when the biblical reference is more general.

- When the meaning of a proper name (or a wordplay inherent in a proper name) is relevant to the message of the text, its meaning is often illuminated with a textual footnote. For example, in Exodus 2:10 the text reads: "The princess named him Moses, for she explained, 'I lifted him out of the water.'" The accompanying footnote reads: "*Moses* sounds like a Hebrew term that means 'to lift out.'"

  Sometimes, when the actual meaning of a name is clear, that meaning is included in parentheses within the text itself. For example, the text at Genesis 16:11 reads: "You are to name him Ishmael *(which means 'God hears'),* for the LORD has heard your cry of distress." Since the original hearers and readers would have instantly understood the meaning of the name "Ishmael," we have provided modern readers with the same information so they can experience the text in a similar way.

- Many words and phrases carry a great deal of cultural meaning that was obvious to the original readers but needs explanation in our own culture. For example, the phrase "they beat their breasts" (Luke 23:48) in ancient times meant that people were very upset, often in mourning. In our translation we chose to translate this phrase dynamically for clarity: "They went home *in deep sorrow.*" Then we included a footnote with the literal Greek, which reads: "Greek *went home beating their breasts.*" In other similar cases, however, we have sometimes chosen to illuminate the existing literal expression to make it immediately understandable. For example, here we might have expanded the literal Greek phrase to read: "They went home beating their breasts *in sorrow.*" If we had done this, we would not have included a textual footnote, since the literal Greek clearly appears in translation.

- Metaphorical language is sometimes difficult for contemporary readers to understand, so at times we have chosen to translate or illuminate the meaning of a metaphor. For example, the ancient poet writes, "Your neck is *like* the tower of David" (Song of Songs 4:4). We have rendered it "Your neck is *as beautiful as* the tower of David" to clarify the intended positive meaning of the simile. Another example comes in Ecclesiastes 12:3, which can be literally rendered: "Remember him . . . when the grinding women cease because they are few, and the women who look through the windows see dimly." We have rendered it: "Remember him before your teeth—your few remaining servants—stop grinding; and before your eyes—the women looking through the windows—see dimly." We clarified such metaphors only when we believed a typical reader might be confused by the literal text.

- When the content of the original language text is poetic in character, we have rendered it in English poetic form. We sought to break lines in ways that clarify and highlight the relationships between phrases of the text. Hebrew poetry often uses parallelism, a literary form where a second phrase (or in some instances a third or fourth) echoes the initial phrase in some way. In Hebrew parallelism, the subsequent parallel phrases continue, while also furthering and sharpening, the thought expressed in the initial line or phrase. Whenever possible, we sought to represent these parallel phrases in natural poetic English.

- The Greek term *hoi Ioudaioi* is literally translated "the Jews" in many English translations. In the Gospel of John, however, this term doesn't always refer to the Jewish people generally. In some contexts, it refers more particularly to the Jewish religious leaders. We have attempted to capture the meaning in these different contexts by using terms such as "the people" (with a footnote: Greek *the Jewish people*) or "the religious leaders," where appropriate.

- One challenge we faced was how to translate accurately the ancient biblical text that was originally written in a context where male-oriented terms were used to refer to humanity generally. We needed to respect the nature of the ancient context while also trying to make the translation clear to a modern audience that tends to read male-oriented language as applying only to males. Often the original text, though using masculine nouns and pronouns, clearly intends that the message be applied to both men and women. A typical example is found in the New Testament letters, where the believers are called "brothers" (*adelphoi*). Yet it is clear from the content of these letters that they were addressed to all the believers—male and female. Thus, we have usually translated this Greek word as "brothers and sisters" in order to represent the historical situation more accurately.

  We have also been sensitive to passages where the text applies generally to human beings or to the human condition. In some instances we have used plural pronouns (they, them) in place of the masculine singular (he, him). For example, a traditional rendering of Proverbs 22:6 is: "Train up a child in the way he should go, and when he is old he will not turn from it." We have rendered it: "Direct your children onto the right path, and when they are older, they will not leave it." At times, we have also replaced third person pronouns with the second person to ensure clarity. A traditional rendering of Proverbs 26:27 is: "He who digs a pit will fall into it, and he who rolls a stone, it will come back on him." We have rendered it: "If you set a trap for others, you will get caught in it yourself. If you roll a boulder down on others, it will crush you instead."

  We should emphasize, however, that all masculine nouns and pronouns used to represent God (for example, "Father") have been maintained without exception. All decisions of this kind have been driven by the concern to reflect accurately the intended meaning of the original texts of Scripture.

Lexical Consistency in Terminology

For the sake of clarity, we have translated certain original-language terms consistently, especially within synoptic passages and for commonly repeated rhetorical phrases, and within certain word categories such as divine names and non-theological technical terminology (e.g., liturgical, legal, cultural, zoological, and botanical terms). For theological terms, we have allowed a greater semantic range of acceptable English words or phrases for a single Hebrew or Greek word. We have avoided some theological terms that are not readily understood by many modern readers. For example, we avoided using words such as "justification" and "sanctification," which are carryovers from Latin translations. In place of these words, we have provided renderings such as "made right with God" and "made holy."

The Spelling of Proper Names
Many individuals in the Bible, especially the Old Testament, are known by more than one name (e.g., Uzziah/Azariah). For the sake of clarity, we have tried to use a single spelling for any one individual, footnoting the literal spelling whenever we differ from it. This is especially helpful in delineating the kings of Israel and Judah. King Joash/Jehoash of Israel has been consistently called Jehoash, while King Joash/Jehoash of Judah is called Joash. A similar distinction has been used to distinguish between Joram/Jehoram of Israel and Joram/Jehoram of Judah. All such decisions were made with the goal of clarifying the text for the reader. When the ancient biblical writers clearly had a theological purpose in their choice of a variant name (e.g., Esh-baal/Ishbosheth), the different names have been maintained with an explanatory footnote.

For the names Jacob and Israel, which are used interchangeably for both the individual patriarch and the nation, we generally render it "Israel" when it refers to the nation and "Jacob" when it refers to the individual. When our rendering of the name differs from the underlying Hebrew text, we provide a textual footnote, which includes this explanation: "The names 'Jacob' and 'Israel' are often interchanged throughout the Old Testament, referring sometimes to the individual patriarch and sometimes to the nation."

The Rendering of Divine Names
All appearances of *'el, 'elohim,* or *'eloah* have been translated "God," except where the context demands the translation "god(s)." We have generally rendered the tetragrammaton (*YHWH*) consistently as "the LORD," utilizing a form with small capitals that is common among English translations. This will distinguish it from the name *'adonai,* which we render "Lord." When *'adonai* and *YHWH* appear together, we have rendered it "Sovereign LORD." This also distinguishes *'adonai YHWH* from cases where *YHWH* appears with *'elohim,* which is rendered "LORD God." When *YH* (the short form of *YHWH*) and *YHWH* appear together, we have rendered it "LORD GOD." When *YHWH* appears with the term *tseba'oth,* we have rendered it "LORD of Heaven's Armies" to translate the meaning of the name. In a few cases, we have utilized the transliteration, *Yahweh,* when the personal character of the name is being invoked in contrast to another divine name or the name of some other god (for example, see Exodus 3:15; 6:2-3).

In the New Testament, the Greek word *christos* has been translated as "Messiah" when the context assumes a Jewish audience. When a Gentile audience can be assumed, *christos* has been translated as "Christ." The Greek word *kurios* is consistently translated "Lord," except that it is translated "LORD" wherever the New Testament text explicitly quotes from the Old Testament, and the text there has it in small capitals.

Textual Footnotes
The New Living Translation provides several kinds of textual footnotes, all designated in the text with an asterisk:

- When for the sake of clarity the NLT renders a difficult or potentially confusing phrase dynamically, we generally give the literal rendering in a textual footnote. This allows the reader to see the literal source of our dynamic rendering and how our translation relates to other more literal translations. These notes are prefaced with "Hebrew," "Aramaic," or "Greek," identifying the language of the underlying source text. For example, in Acts 2:42 we translated the literal "breaking of bread" (from the Greek) as "the Lord's Supper" to clarify that this verse refers to the ceremonial practice of the church rather than just an ordinary meal. Then we attached a footnote to "the Lord's Supper," which reads: "Greek *the breaking of bread.*"

- Textual footnotes are also used to show alternative renderings, prefaced with the word "Or." These normally occur for passages where an aspect of the meaning is debated. On occasion, we also provide notes on words or phrases that represent a departure from long-standing tradition. These notes are prefaced with "Traditionally rendered." For example, the footnote to the translation "serious skin disease" at Leviticus 13:2 says: "Traditionally rendered *leprosy*. The Hebrew word used throughout this passage is used to describe various skin diseases."
- When our translators follow a textual variant that differs significantly from our standard Hebrew or Greek texts (listed earlier), we document that difference with a footnote. We also footnote cases when the NLT excludes a passage that is included in the Greek text known as the *Textus Receptus* (and familiar to readers through its translation in the King James Version). In such cases, we offer a translation of the excluded text in a footnote, even though it is generally recognized as a later addition to the Greek text and not part of the original Greek New Testament.
- All Old Testament passages that are quoted in the New Testament are identified by a textual footnote at the New Testament location. When the New Testament clearly quotes from the Greek translation of the Old Testament, and when it differs significantly in wording from the Hebrew text, we also place a textual footnote at the Old Testament location. This note includes a rendering of the Greek version, along with a cross-reference to the New Testament passage(s) where it is cited (for example, see notes on Psalms 8:2; 53:3; Proverbs 3:12).
- Some textual footnotes provide cultural and historical information on places, things, and people in the Bible that are probably obscure to modern readers. Such notes should aid the reader in understanding the message of the text. For example, in Acts 12:1, "King Herod" is named in this translation as "King Herod Agrippa" and is identified in a footnote as being "the nephew of Herod Antipas and a grandson of Herod the Great."
- When the meaning of a proper name (or a wordplay inherent in a proper name) is relevant to the meaning of the text, it is either illuminated with a textual footnote or included within parentheses in the text itself. For example, the footnote concerning the name "Eve" at Genesis 3:20 reads: "*Eve* sounds like a Hebrew term that means 'to give life.'" This wordplay in the Hebrew illuminates the meaning of the text, which goes on to say that Eve "would be the mother of all who live."

As WE SUBMIT this translation for publication, we recognize that any translation of the Scriptures is subject to limitations and imperfections. Anyone who has attempted to communicate the richness of God's Word into another language will realize it is impossible to make a perfect translation. Recognizing these limitations, we sought God's guidance and wisdom throughout this project. Now we pray that he will accept our efforts and use this translation for the benefit of the church and of all people.

We pray that the New Living Translation will overcome some of the barriers of history, culture, and language that have kept people from reading and understanding God's Word. We hope that readers unfamiliar with the Bible will find the words clear and easy to understand and that readers well versed in the Scriptures will gain a fresh perspective. We pray that readers will gain insight and wisdom for living, but most of all that they will meet the God of the Bible and be forever changed by knowing him.

The Bible Translation Committee
October 2007

WHY THE
LIFE APPLICATION STUDY BIBLE
IS UNIQUE

Have you ever opened your Bible and asked the following:

- What does this passage really mean?
- How does it apply to my life?
- Why does some of the Bible seem irrelevant?
- What do these ancient cultures have to do with today?
- I love God; why can't I understand what he is saying to me through his word?
- What's going on in the lives of these Bible people?

Many Christians do not read the Bible regularly. Why? Because in the pressures of daily living they cannot find a connection between the timeless principles of Scripture and the ever-present problems of day-by-day living.

God urges us to apply his word (Isaiah 42:23; 1 Corinthians 10:11; 2 Thessalonians 3:4), but too often we stop at accumulating Bible knowledge. This is why the *Life Application Study Bible* was developed—to show how to put into practice what we have learned.

Applying God's word is a vital part of one's relationship with God; it is the evidence that we are obeying him. The difficulty in applying the Bible is not with the Bible itself, but with the reader's inability to bridge the gap between the past and present, the conceptual and practical. When we don't or can't do this, spiritual dryness, shallowness, and indifference are the results.

The words of Scripture itself cry out to us, "But don't just listen to God's word. You must do what it says. Otherwise, you are only fooling yourselves" (James 1:22). The *Life Application Study Bible* helps us to obey God's word. Developed by an interdenominational team of pastors, scholars, family counselors, and a national organization dedicated to promoting God's word and spreading the gospel, the *Life Application Study Bible* took many years to complete. All the work was reviewed by several renowned theologians under the directorship of Dr. Kenneth Kantzer.

The *Life Application Study Bible* does what a good resource Bible should: It helps you understand the context of a passage, gives important background and historical information, explains difficult words and phrases, and helps you see the interrelationship of Scripture. But it does much more. The *Life Application Study Bible* goes deeper into God's word, helping you discover the timeless truth being communicated, see the relevance for your life, and make a personal application. While some study Bibles attempt application, over 75 percent of this Bible is application oriented. The notes answer the questions "So what?" and "What does this passage mean to me, my family, my friends, my job, my neighborhood, my church, my country?"

Imagine reading a familiar passage of Scripture and gaining fresh insight, as if it were the first time you had ever read it. How much richer your life would be if you left each Bible reading with a new perspective and a small change for the better. A small change every day adds up to a changed life—and that is the very purpose of Scripture.

WHAT IS APPLICATION?

The best way to define application is to first determine what it is *not*. Application is *not* just accumulating knowledge. Accumulating knowledge helps us discover and understand facts and concepts, but it stops there. History is filled with philosophers who knew what the Bible said but failed to apply it to their lives, keeping them from believing and changing. Many think that understanding is the end goal of Bible study, but it is really only the beginning.

Application is *not* just illustration. Illustration only tells us how someone else handled a similar situation. While we may empathize with that person, we still have little direction for our personal situation.

Application is *not* just making a passage "relevant." Making the Bible relevant only helps us to see that the same lessons that were true in Bible times are true today; it does not show us how to apply them to the problems and pressures of our individual lives.

What, then, is application? Application begins by knowing and understanding God's word and its timeless truths. *But you cannot stop there.* If you do, God's word may not change your life, and it may become dull, difficult, tedious, and tiring. A good application focuses the truth of God's word, shows the reader what to do about what is being read, and motivates the reader to respond to what God is teaching. All three are essential to application.

Application is putting into practice what we already know (see Mark 4:24 and Hebrews 5:14) and answering the question "So what?" by confronting us with the right questions and motivating us to take action (see 1 John 2:5-6 and James 2:26). Application is deeply personal—unique for each individual. It makes a relevant truth a personal truth and involves developing a strategy and action plan to live your life in harmony with the Bible. It is the biblical "how to" of life.

You may ask, "How can your application notes be relevant to my life?" Each application note has three parts: (1) an *explanation*, which ties the note directly to the Scripture passage and sets up the truth that is being taught; (2) the *bridge*, which explains the timeless truth and makes it relevant for today; (3) the *application*, which shows you how to take the timeless truth and apply it to your personal situation. No note, by itself, can apply Scripture directly to your life. It can only teach, direct, lead, guide, inspire, recommend, and urge. It can give you the resources and direction you need to apply the Bible, but only you can take these resources and put them into practice.

A good note, therefore, should not only give you knowledge and understanding but point you to application. Before you buy any kind of resource study Bible, you should evaluate the notes and ask the following questions: (1) Does the note contain enough information to help me understand the point of the Scripture passage? (2) Does the note assume I know more than I do? (3) Does the note avoid denominational bias? (4) Do the notes touch most of life's experiences? (5) Does the note help me apply God's word?

FEATURES OF THE
LIFE APPLICATION STUDY BIBLE

NOTES

In addition to providing the reader with many application notes, the *Life Application Study Bible* also offers several kinds of explanatory notes, which help the reader understand culture, history, context, difficult-to-understand passages, background, places, theological concepts, and the relationship of various passages in Scripture to other passages.

BOOK INTRODUCTIONS

Each book introduction is divided into several easy-to-find parts:

Timeline. A guide that puts the Bible book into its historical setting. It lists the key events and the dates when they occurred.

Vital Statistics. A list of straight facts about the book—those pieces of information you need to know at a glance.

Overview. A summary of the book with general lessons and applications that can be learned from the book as a whole.

Blueprint. The outline of the book. It is printed in easy-to-understand language and is designed for easy memorization. To the right of each main heading is a key lesson that is taught in that particular section.

Megathemes. A section that gives the main themes of the Bible book, explains their significance, and then tells you why they are still important for us today.

Map. If included, this shows the key places found in that book and retells the story of the book from a geographical point of view.

OUTLINE

The *Life Application Study Bible* has a new, custom-made outline that was designed specifically from an application point of view. Several unique features should be noted:

1. To avoid confusion and to aid memory work, the book outline has only three levels for headings. Main outline heads are marked with a capital letter. Subheads are marked by a number. Minor explanatory heads have no letter or number.

2. Each main outline head marked by a letter also has a brief paragraph below it summarizing the Bible text and offering a general application.

3. Parallel passages are listed where they apply.

PERSONALITY PROFILES

Among the unique features of this Bible are the profiles of key Bible people, including their strengths and weaknesses, greatest accomplishments and mistakes, and key lessons from their lives.

MAPS

The *Life Application Study Bible* has a thorough and comprehensive Bible atlas built right into the book. There are two kinds of maps: a book-introduction map, telling the story of the book, and thumbnail maps in the notes, plotting most geographic movements.

CHARTS AND DIAGRAMS

Many charts and diagrams are included to help the reader better visualize difficult concepts or relationships. Most charts not only present the needed information but show the significance of the information as well.

CROSS-REFERENCES

An updated, exhaustive cross-reference system in the margins of the Bible text helps the reader find related passages quickly.

TEXTUAL NOTES

Directly related to the text of the New Living Translation, the textual notes provide explanations on certain wording in the translation, alternate translations, and information about readings in the ancient manuscripts.

HIGHLIGHTED NOTES

In each Bible study lesson, you will be asked to read specific notes as part of your preparation. These notes have each been highlighted by a bullet (•) so that you can find them easily.

1 & 2 THESSALONIANS

1 THESSALONIANS

SLOWLY they walk, one by one, scattering the leaves and trampling the grass under measured and heavy steps. The minister's words still echoing in their minds, they hear workmen moving toward the terrible place, preparing to cover the casket of their loved one. Death, the enemy, has torn the bonded relationships of family and friends, leaving only memories . . . and tears . . . and loneliness.

But like a golden shaft of sun piercing the winter sky, a singular truth shatters the oppressive gloom: Death is not the end! Christ is the victor over death, and there is the hope of resurrection through him.

As with every member of the human family, first-century Christians came face to face with their mortality. Many of them met early deaths at the hands of those who hated Christ and all allied with him. Whether at the hands of zealous Jews (like Paul before his conversion), angry Greeks, or ruthless Roman authorities, persecution included stonings, beatings, crucifixions, torture, and death. To be a follower of Christ meant to give up everything.

Paul established the church in Thessalonica during his second missionary journey (about A.D. 51). He wrote this letter a short time later to encourage the young believers there. He wanted to assure them of his love, to praise them for their faithfulness during persecution, and to remind them of their hope—the sure return of their Lord and Savior.

Paul begins this letter with a note of affirmation, thanking God for the strong faith and good reputation of the Thessalonians (1:1–10). Then Paul reviews their relationship—how he and his companions brought the gospel to them (2:1–12), how they accepted the message (2:13–16), and how he longed to be with them again (2:17–20). Because of his concern, he had sent Timothy to encourage them in their faith (3:1–13).

Paul then presents the core of his message—exhortation and comfort. He challenges them to please God in their daily living by avoiding sexual immorality (4:1–8), loving each other (4:9, 10), and living as good citizens in a sinful world (4:11, 12).

Paul comforts the Thessalonians by reminding them of the hope of resurrection (4:13–18). Then he warns them to be prepared at all times, for Jesus Christ could return at any moment. When Christ returns, those Christians who are alive and those who have died will be raised to new life (5:1–11).

Paul then gives the Thessalonians a handful of reminders on how to prepare themselves for the Second Coming: Warn the lazy (5:14), encourage the timid (5:14), help the weak (5:14), be patient with everyone (5:14), be kind to everyone (5:15), be joyful always (5:16), pray continually (5:17), give thanks (5:18), test everything that is taught (5:20, 21), and avoid evil (5:22). Paul concludes his letter with two benedictions and a request for prayer.

As you read this letter, listen carefully to Paul's practical advice for Christian living. And when burdened by grief and overwhelmed by sorrow, take hope in the reality of Christ's return, resurrection, and eternal life!

VITAL STATISTICS

PURPOSE:
To strengthen the Thessalonian Christians in their faith and give them the assurance of Christ's return

AUTHOR:
Paul

ORIGINAL AUDIENCE:
The church at Thessalonica

DATE WRITTEN:
Approximately A.D. 51 from Corinth; one of Paul's earliest letters

SETTING:
The church at Thessalonica was very young, having been established only two or three years before this letter was written. The Thessalonian Christians needed to mature in their faith. In addition, there was a misunderstanding concerning Christ's second coming—some thought Christ would return immediately; thus, they were confused when their loved ones died because they expected Christ to return beforehand. Also, believers were being persecuted.

KEY VERSE:
"For since we believe that Jesus died and was raised to life again, we also believe that when Jesus returns, God will bring back with him the believers who have died" (4:14).

KEY PEOPLE:
Paul, Timothy, Silas

KEY PLACE:
Thessalonica

SPECIAL FEATURES:
Paul received from Timothy a favorable report about the Thessalonians. However, Paul wrote this letter to correct their misconceptions about the resurrection and the second coming of Christ.

THE BLUEPRINT

1. Faithfulness to the Lord
   (1:1—3:13)
2. Watchfulness for the Lord
   (4:1—5:28)

Paul and his companions were faithful to bring the gospel to the Thessalonians in the midst of persecution. The Thessalonians had only recently become Christians, and yet they had remained faithful to the Lord, despite the fact that the apostles were not with them. Others have been faithful in bringing God's Word to us. We must remain faithful and live in the expectation that Christ will return at any time.

MEGATHEMES

THEME	EXPLANATION	IMPORTANCE
Persecution	Paul and the new Christians at Thessalonica experienced persecution because of their faith in Christ. We can expect trials and troubles as well. We need to stand firm in our faith in the midst of trials, being strengthened by the Holy Spirit.	The Holy Spirit helps us to remain strong in faith, able to show genuine love to others and maintain our moral character even when we are being persecuted, slandered, or oppressed.
Paul's Ministry	Paul expressed his concern for this church even while he was being slandered. Paul's commitment to share the gospel in spite of difficult circumstances is a model we should follow.	Paul not only delivered his message, but gave of himself. In our ministries, we must become like Paul—faithful and bold, yet sensitive and self-sacrificing.
Hope	One day all believers, both those who are alive and those who have died, will be united with Christ. To those Christians who die before Christ's return, there is hope—the hope of the resurrection of the body.	If we believe in Christ, we will live with him forever. All those who belong to Jesus Christ—from throughout history—will be present with him at his second coming. We can be confident that we will be with loved ones who have trusted in Christ.
Being Prepared	No one knows the time of Christ's return. We are to live moral and holy lives, ever watchful for his coming. Believers must not neglect daily responsibilities, but always work and live to please the Lord.	The gospel is not only what we believe but also what we must live. The Holy Spirit leads us in faithfulness, so we can avoid lust and fraud. Live as though you expect Christ's return at any time. Don't be caught unprepared.

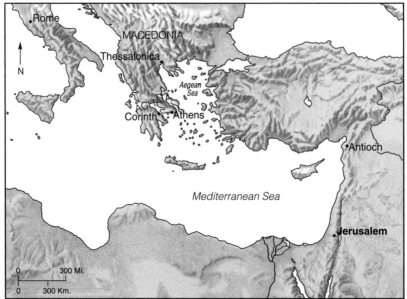

LOCATION OF THESSALONICA

Paul visited Thessalonica on his second and third missionary journeys. It was a seaport and trade center located on the Egnatian Way, a busy international highway. Paul probably wrote his two letters to the Thessalonians from Corinth.

1. Faithfulness to the Lord

Greetings from Paul

1:1
Acts 17:1
2 Thes 1:1

1 This letter is from Paul, Silas,* and Timothy.

We are writing to the church in Thessalonica, to you who belong to God the Father and the Lord Jesus Christ.

May God give you grace and peace.

The Faith of the Thessalonian Believers

1:3
1 Cor 13:13
2 Thes 1:11

²We always thank God for all of you and pray for you constantly. ³As we pray to our God and Father about you, we think of your faithful work, your loving deeds, and the enduring hope you have because of our Lord Jesus Christ.

1:4
2 Thes 2:13
2 Pet 1:10
1:5
1 Cor 2:4-5; 4:20
2 Thes 3:7
1:6
Acts 17:1-9
1 Cor 4:16

⁴We know, dear brothers and sisters,* that God loves you and has chosen you to be his own people. ⁵For when we brought you the Good News, it was not only with words but also with power, for the Holy Spirit gave you full assurance* that what we said was true. And you know of our concern for you from the way we lived when we were with you. ⁶So you received the message with joy from the Holy Spirit in spite of the severe suffering it brought you. In this way, you imitated both us and the Lord. ⁷As a result, you have become an example to all the believers in Greece—throughout both Macedonia and Achaia.*

1:1 Greek *Silvanus*, the Greek form of the name.   **1:4** Greek *brothers*.   **1:5** Or *with the power of the Holy Spirit, so you can have full assurance.*   **1:7** *Macedonia* and *Achaia* were the northern and southern regions of Greece.

• **1:1** Paul and his companions probably arrived in Thessalonica in the early summer of A.D. 50. They planted the first Christian church in that city, but had to leave in a hurry because their lives were threatened (Acts 17:1-10). At the first opportunity, probably when he stopped at Corinth, Paul sent Timothy back to Thessalonica to see how the new believers were doing. Timothy returned to Paul with good news: The Christians in Thessalonica were remaining firm in the faith and were unified. But the Thessalonians did have some questions about their new faith. Paul had not had time to answer all their questions during his brief visit, and in the meantime, other questions had arisen. So Paul wrote this letter to answer their questions and to commend them on their faithfulness to Christ.

• **1:1** For more information on Paul, see his Profile in Acts 9, p. 1837. Silas accompanied Paul on his second missionary journey (Acts 15:36—17:15). He helped Paul establish the church in Thessalonica (Acts 17:1-9). He is also mentioned in 2 Corinthians 1:19, 2 Thessalonians 1:1, and in 1 Peter 5:12. Silas's Profile is found in Acts 16, p. 1859. Timothy's Profile is in 1 Timothy 2, p. 2059.

• **1:1** Thessalonica was the capital and largest city (about 200,000 population) of the Roman province of Macedonia. The most important Roman highway (the Egnatian Way)—extending from Rome all the way to the Orient—went through Thessalonica. This highway, along with the city's thriving seaport, made Thessalonica one of the wealthiest and most flourishing trade centers in the Roman Empire. Recognized as a free city, Thessalonica was allowed self-rule and was exempt from most of the restrictions placed by Rome on other cities in the empire. With its international flavor, however, came many pagan religions and cultural influences that challenged the faith of the young Christians there.

• **1:3** The Thessalonians had stood firm when they were persecuted (1:6; 3:1-4, 7, 8). Paul commended these young Christians for their faithful work, loving deeds, and anticipation of the Lord's return. These characteristics are the marks of effective Christians in any age.

1:4 Paul reminded the Thessalonians of their status as God's "chosen" ones. Very few issues cause more confusion and even arguments among Christians than the issue of election (being chosen by God). It is difficult to simultaneously embrace God's sovereignty in choosing us and our human responsibility in choosing to follow him. Even though we may not be able to completely comprehend how these two truths can coexist, we can say the following: *Being chosen* comes from the heart of God (not our

minds), should be an incentive to please God (not ignore him), and should give birth to gratitude (not complacency). *Human responsibility* requires that we actively confess Christ as Lord, focus on living to please him, and share the gospel with others.

God's choice of us energizes us to obey and to serve. Our choice of God challenges us to build lives worthy of him. As you consider God's divine selection of you, how do you respond?

1:5 The Good News came "with power"; it had a powerful effect on the Thessalonians. Whenever the Bible is heard and obeyed, lives are changed! Christianity is more than a collection of interesting facts; it is the power of God to everyone who believes. What has God's power done in your life since you first believed?

1:5 The Holy Spirit changes people when they believe the Good News. When we tell others about Christ, we must depend on the Holy Spirit to open their eyes and convince them that they need salvation. God's power—not our cleverness or persuasion—changes people. Without the work of the Holy Spirit, our words are meaningless. The Holy Spirit not only convicts people of sin but also assures them of the truth of the Good News. (For more information on the Holy Spirit, see John 14:23-26; 15:26, 27; and the notes on John 3:6 and Acts 1:5.)

1:5 Paul wrote, "And you know of our concern for you from the way we lived when we were with you." The Thessalonians had seen that what Paul, Silas, and Timothy were preaching was true because these men had lived it. Does your life confirm or contradict what you say you believe?

• **1:6** The message of salvation, though welcomed with great joy, brought the Thessalonians severe suffering because it led to persecution from both Jews and Gentiles (3:2-4; Acts 17:5). Many believers today think that pain is the exception in the Christian life. When suffering occurs, they say, "Why me?" They feel as though God deserted them, or perhaps they accuse him of not being as dependable as they thought he should be. In reality, the world is sinful, so even believers suffer. God allows some Christians to become martyrs for the faith, and he allows others to survive persecution. Rather than asking, "Why me?" we should ask, "Why not me?" Our faith and the values of this world are on a collision course. If we expect pain and suffering to come, we will not be shocked when they occur. We can take comfort in knowing that Jesus also suffered. He understands our fears, our weaknesses, and our disappointments (Hebrews 2:16-18; 4:14-16). He promised never to leave us (Matthew 28:18-20), and he intercedes on our behalf (Hebrews 7:24, 25). In times of pain, persecution, or suffering, trust confidently in Christ.

8And now the word of the Lord is ringing out from you to people everywhere, even beyond Macedonia and Achaia, for wherever we go we find people telling us about your faith in God. We don't need to tell them about it, 9for they keep talking about the wonderful welcome you gave us and how you turned away from idols to serve the living and true God. 10And they speak of how you are looking forward to the coming of God's Son from heaven—Jesus, whom God raised from the dead. He is the one who has rescued us from the terrors of the coming judgment.

Paul Remembers His Visit

2 You yourselves know, dear brothers and sisters,* that our visit to you was not a failure. 2You know how badly we had been treated at Philippi just before we came to you and how much we suffered there. Yet our God gave us the courage to declare his Good News to you boldly, in spite of great opposition. 3So you can see we were not preaching with any deceit or impure motives or trickery.

4For we speak as messengers approved by God to be entrusted with the Good News. Our purpose is to please God, not people. He alone examines the motives of our hearts. 5Never once did we try to win you with flattery, as you well know. And God is our witness that we were not pretending to be your friends just to get your money! 6As for human praise, we have never sought it from you or anyone else.

7As apostles of Christ we certainly had a right to make some demands of you, but instead we were like children* among you. Or we were like a mother feeding and caring for her own children. 8We loved you so much that we shared with you not only God's Good News but our own lives, too.

9Don't you remember, dear brothers and sisters, how hard we worked among you? Night and day we toiled to earn a living so that we would not be a burden to any of you as we preached God's Good News to you. 10You yourselves are our witnesses—and so is God—that we were devout and honest and faultless toward all of you believers. 11And you know that we

1:8
Rom 1:8
2 Thes 3:1
1:9
Acts 14:15
1 Cor 12:2
1:10
Phil 3:20
1 Thes 5:9
Titus 2:13
Heb 9:28
Rev 1:7
2:1
1 Thes 1:5, 9
2:2
Acts 16:22; 17:2
Phil 1:30
2:3
2 Cor 4:2
2 Pet 1:16
2:4
Gal 1:10
1 Tim 1:11
2:5
Acts 20:33
2:7
2 Tim 2:24
2:8
2 Cor 12:15
2:9
Acts 18:3
2 Cor 11:9
2 Thes 3:8
2:10
1 Thes 1:5
2:11
1 Cor 4:14

2:1 Greek *brothers;* also in 2:9, 14, 17. **2:7** Some manuscripts read *we were gentle.*

• **1:9, 10** All of us should respond to the Good News as the Thessalonians did: *Turn* to God, *serve* God, and *look forward* to the return of his Son, Christ, from heaven. We should turn from sin to God because Christ is coming to judge the earth. We should be fervent in our service because we have little time before Christ returns. We should be prepared for Christ to return because we don't know when he will come.

• **1:10** Paul emphasized Christ's second coming throughout this book. Because the Thessalonian church was being persecuted, Paul encouraged them to look forward to the deliverance that Christ would bring. A believer's hope is in the return of Jesus (Titus 2:13). Our perspective on life remains incomplete without this hope. Just as surely as Christ was raised from the dead and ascended into heaven, he will return (Acts 1:11).

• **2:1, 2** "Our visit to you" refers to Paul's first visit to Thessalonica recorded in Acts 17:1-9. The Thessalonians knew that Paul had been imprisoned in Philippi just prior to coming to Thessalonica (see Acts 16:11–17:1). Fear of imprisonment did not keep Paul from preaching the Good News. If God wants us to do something, he will give us the strength and courage to boldly speak out for him despite any obstacles that may come our way. Boldness is not reckless impulsiveness. Boldness requires courage to press through fears and do what is right. How can we be more bold? Like the apostles, we need to pray for that kind of courage. To gain boldness, you can pray for the Holy Spirit's power, look for opportunities to talk about Christ, and start right where you are being bolder in even small ways.

2:3 This pointed statement may be a response to accusations from the Jewish leaders who had stirred up the crowds (Acts 17:5). Paul did not seek money, fame, or popularity by sharing the Good News. He demonstrated the sincerity of his motives by showing that he and Silas had suffered for sharing the Good News in Philippi. People become involved in ministry for a variety of reasons, not all of them good or pure. When their bad motives are exposed, all of Christ's work suffers. When you get involved in ministry, do so out of love for Christ and others.

• **2:4-8** In trying to persuade people, we may be tempted to alter our position just enough to make our message more palatable or to use flattery or praise. Paul never changed his *message* to make it more acceptable, but he did tailor his *methods* to each audience. Although our presentation must be altered to be appropriate to the situation, the truth of the Good News must never be compromised.

2:5 It's disgusting to hear a person butter up someone. Flattery is phony, and it covers up a person's real intentions. Christians should not be flatterers. Those who proclaim God's truth have a special responsibility to be honest. Are you honest and straightforward in your words and actions? Or do you tell people what they want to hear in order to get what you want or to get ahead?

2:6-8 When Paul was with the Thessalonians, he didn't flatter them, seek their praise, or become a burden to them. He and Silas completely focused their efforts on presenting God's message of salvation to the Thessalonians. This was important! The Thessalonian believers had their lives changed by God, not Paul; it was Christ's message they believed, not Paul's. When we witness for Christ, our focus should not be on the impression we make. As true ministers of Christ, we should point to him, not to ourselves.

2:7 That Paul and his companions "were like children" among the Thessalonians does not mean they were immature or untrained. Rather, Paul was making the point that, like children, they were honest, straightforward, and without guile in their presentation of the gospel and of their lives.

• **2:9** Although Paul had the right to receive financial support from the people he taught, he supported himself as a tentmaker (Acts 18:3) so that he wouldn't be a burden to the new Thessalonian believers.

2:11 No loving father would neglect the safety of his children, allowing them to walk into circumstances that might be harmful or fatal. In the same way, we must take new believers under our wing until they are mature enough to stand firm in their faith. We must help new Christians become strong enough to influence others for the sake of the Good News.

2:12
Eph 4:1
Col 1:10
1 Pet 1:15

2:13
1 Thes 1:2
2 Thes 2:13

2:14
Acts 17:5
1 Thes 1:6

2:15
Luke 24:20
Acts 2:23; 7:52

2:16
Matt 23:32-33
Acts 13:45, 50;
17:5; 20:3; 21:27;
24:9

2:17
1 Cor 5:3
1 Thes 3:10

2:18
Rom 1:13; 15:22

2:19
Phil 2:16

2:20
2 Cor 1:14

treated each of you as a father treats his own children. ¹²We pleaded with you, encouraged you, and urged you to live your lives in a way that God would consider worthy. For he called you to share in his Kingdom and glory.

¹³Therefore, we never stop thanking God that when you received his message from us, you didn't think of our words as mere human ideas. You accepted what we said as the very word of God—which, of course, it is. And this word continues to work in you who believe.

¹⁴And then, dear brothers and sisters, you suffered persecution from your own country-men. In this way, you imitated the believers in God's churches in Judea who, because of their belief in Christ Jesus, suffered from their own people, the Jews. ¹⁵For some of the Jews killed the prophets, and some even killed the Lord Jesus. Now they have persecuted us, too. They fail to please God and work against all humanity ¹⁶as they try to keep us from preaching the Good News of salvation to the Gentiles. By doing this, they continue to pile up their sins. But the anger of God has caught up with them at last.

Timothy's Good Report about the Church

¹⁷Dear brothers and sisters, after we were separated from you for a little while (though our hearts never left you), we tried very hard to come back because of our intense longing to see you again. ¹⁸We wanted very much to come to you, and I, Paul, tried again and again, but Satan prevented us. ¹⁹After all, what gives us hope and joy, and what will be our proud reward and crown as we stand before our Lord Jesus when he returns? It is you! ²⁰Yes, you are our pride and joy.

THE EVENTS OF CHRIST'S RETURN

1. Christ will return visibly, with a commanding shout.
2. There will be an unmistakable call from an angel.
3. There will be a trumpet fanfare such as has never been heard.
4. Believers in Christ who are dead will rise from their graves.
5. Believers who are alive will be caught up in the clouds to meet the Lord.

While Christians have often disagreed about what events will lead up to the return of Christ, there has been less disagreement about what will happen once Christ does return.

2:12 By his words and example, Paul encouraged the Thessalonians to live in a way God would consider worthy. Is there anything about your daily life that would embarrass God? What do people think of God from watching you?

• **2:13** Paul said that the word of God continued to work in the believers' lives. Paul knew that God's words are not mere sermons or documents but a real source of transforming power. This Bible you hold in your hands is full of real and living power. Its words are transforming lives all over the world every day. Read it. Encourage fellow believers to read it. Encourage non-Christian friends to read it. All who do so, truly seeking to learn, will be touched by its power. They will never be the same.

• **2:14** Just as the Jewish Christians in Jerusalem were persecuted by other Jews, so the Gentile Christians in Thessalonica were persecuted by their fellow Gentiles. Persecution is discouraging, especially when it comes from your own people. When you take a stand for Christ, you may face opposition, disapproval, and ridicule from your neighbors, friends, and even family members.

• **2:14** When Paul refers to the Jews, he is talking about certain Jews who opposed his preaching of the Good News. He does not mean all Jews. Many of Paul's converts were Jewish. Paul himself was a Jew (2 Corinthians 11:22).

2:15 Having believed the Good News and accepted new life in Christ, apparently many Thessalonians thought that they would be protected from death until Christ returned. Then, when believers began to die under persecution, some Thessalonian Christians started to question their faith. Many of Paul's comments throughout this letter were addressed to these people, as he explained what happens when believers die (see 4:13ff).

• **2:15, 16** Why were so many Jews opposed to Christianity? (1) Although the Jewish religion had been declared legal by the Roman government, it still had a tenuous relationship with the government. At this time, Christianity was viewed as a sect of Judaism. The Jews were afraid that reprisals leveled against the Christians might be expanded to include them. (2) The Jewish leaders thought Jesus was a false prophet, and they didn't want his teachings to spread. (3) The leaders feared that if many Jews were drawn away, their own political position might be weakened. (4) Jews were proud of their special status as God's chosen people and resented the fact that Gentiles could be full members within the Christian church.

• **2:18** Satan is real. He is called "the god of this world" (2 Corinthians 4:4) and "the commander of the powers in the unseen world" (Ephesians 2:2). We don't know exactly what hindered Paul from returning to Thessalonica—opposition, illness, travel complications, or a direct attack by Satan—but Satan worked in some way to keep him away. Many of the difficulties that prevent us from accomplishing God's work can be attributed to Satan (see Ephesians 6:12).

2:20 The ultimate reward for Paul's ministry was not money, prestige, or fame, but new believers whose lives had been changed by God through the preaching of the Good News. This was why he longed to see them. No matter what ministry God has given to you, your highest reward and greatest joy should be those who come to believe in Christ and are growing in him.

3 Finally, when we could stand it no longer, we decided to stay alone in Athens, ²and we sent Timothy to visit you. He is our brother and God's co-worker* in proclaiming the Good News of Christ. We sent him to strengthen you, to encourage you in your faith, ³and to keep you from being shaken by the troubles you were going through. But you know that we are destined for such troubles. ⁴Even while we were with you, we warned you that troubles would soon come—and they did, as you well know. ⁵That is why, when I could bear it no longer, I sent Timothy to find out whether your faith was still strong. I was afraid that the tempter had gotten the best of you and that our work had been useless.

⁶But now Timothy has just returned, bringing us good news about your faith and love. He reports that you always remember our visit with joy and that you want to see us as much as we want to see you. ⁷So we have been greatly encouraged in the midst of our troubles and suffering, dear brothers and sisters,* because you have remained strong in your faith. ⁸It gives us new life to know that you are standing firm in the Lord.

⁹How we thank God for you! Because of you we have great joy as we enter God's presence. ¹⁰Night and day we pray earnestly for you, asking God to let us see you again to fill the gaps in your faith.

¹¹May God our Father and our Lord Jesus bring us to you very soon. ¹²And may the Lord make your love for one another and for all people grow and overflow, just as our love for you overflows. ¹³May he, as a result, make your hearts strong, blameless, and holy as you stand before God our Father when our Lord Jesus comes again with all his holy people. Amen.

3:1 Acts 17:15
3:2 Acts 16:1-3
3:3 2 Tim 3:12
3:4 1 Thes 2:14
3:5 Matt 4:3 Phil 2:16
3:6 Acts 18:5
3:7 2 Thes 1:4
3:8 1 Cor 16:13
3:10 1 Thes 2:16-17 2 Tim 1:3
3:12 Phil 1:9
3:13 Zech 14:5 1 Cor 1:8 1 Thes 1:7, 10; 2:19

2. Watchfulness for the Lord

Live to Please God

4 Finally, dear brothers and sisters,* we urge you in the name of the Lord Jesus to live in a way that pleases God, as we have taught you. You live this way already, and we encourage you to do so even more. ²For you remember what we taught you by the authority of the Lord Jesus.

4:1 Eph 4:1 2 Thes 3:6
4:2 2 Thes 3:4

3:2 Other manuscripts read *and God's servant;* still others read *and a co-worker,* or *and a servant and co-worker for God,* or *and God's servant and our co-worker.*   **3:7** Greek *brothers.*   **4:1** Greek *brothers;* also in 4:10, 13.

• **3:1-3** Some think that troubles are always caused by sin or a lack of faith. Trials may be a part of God's plan for believers. Experiencing problems and persecutions can build character (James 1:2-4), perseverance (Romans 5:3-5), and sensitivity toward others who also face trouble (2 Corinthians 1:3-7). Problems are unavoidable for God's people. Your troubles may be a sign of effective Christian living.

3:2-5 Because Paul could not return to Thessalonica (2:18), he sent Timothy as his representative. According to Acts 17:10, Paul left Thessalonica and went to Berea. When trouble broke out in Berea, some Christians took Paul to Athens, while Silas and Timothy stayed behind (Acts 17:13-15). Then Paul directed Silas and Timothy to join him in Athens. Later, Paul sent Timothy to encourage the Thessalonian Christians to be strong in their faith in the face of persecution and other troubles.

• **3:4** Some people turn to God with the hope of escaping suffering on earth. But God doesn't promise that. Instead, he gives us power to grow through our sufferings. The Christian life involves obedience to Christ despite temptations and hardships.

• **3:5** Satan ("the tempter") is the most powerful of the evil spirits. His power can affect both the spiritual world (Ephesians 2:1-3; 6:10-12) and the physical world (2 Corinthians 12:7-10). Satan even tempted Jesus (Matthew 4:1-11). But Jesus defeated Satan when he died on the cross for our sins and rose again to bring us new life. At the proper time God will overthrow Satan forever (Revelation 20:7-10).

• **3:7, 8** During persecution or pressure, believers should encourage one another. Christians who stand firm in the Lord are an encouragement to ministers and teachers (who can see the benefit of their work in those who remain faithful) and also an encouragement to those who are new in their faith (who can learn from the steadfastness of the mature).

3:9, 10 It brings great joy to a Christian to see another person come to faith in Christ and mature in that faith. Paul experienced this joy countless times. He thanked God for those who had come to know Christ and for their strong faith. He also prayed for their continued growth. If new Christians have brought you joy, thank God for them and support them as they continue to grow in the faith. Likewise, have you benefited from the ministry of others? Has someone's guidance and faithfulness stimulated you to grow in Christ? Consider how you may bring some word of encouragement or some thoughtful gift. Let that important person know that you have followed his or her example by being faithful to Christ.

3:11 Paul wanted to return to Thessalonica. We have no record that he was able to do so; but when he was traveling through Asia on his third journey, he was joined by Aristarchus and Secundus, who were from Thessalonica (Acts 20:4, 5).

3:12 If we are full of God's love, it will overflow to others. It's not enough merely to be courteous to others; we must actively and persistently show love to them. Our love should be growing continually. If your capacity to love has remained unchanged for some time, ask God to fill you again with his never-ending supply. Then look for opportunities to let his love spill over in refreshment to others.

3:13 "When our Lord Jesus comes again with all his holy people" refers to the second coming of Christ when he will establish his eternal Kingdom. At that time, Christ will gather all believers, those who have died and those who are alive, into one united family under his rule. All believers from all times, including these Thessalonian believers, will be with Christ in his Kingdom.

• **4:1-8** Sexual standards were very low in the Roman Empire, and in many societies today, they are not any higher. The temptation to engage in sexual intercourse outside the marriage relationship has always been powerful. Giving in to that temptation can have disastrous results. Sexual sins always hurt someone: individuals, families, businesses, churches. Sexual desires and activities must be placed under Christ's control. God created sex for procreation and pleasure and as an expression of love between a husband

4:3
Heb 10:10
1 Pet 1:16

4:4
1 Cor 7:2

4:7
Lev 11:44
2 Thes 2:13-14
1 Pet 1:15

4:8
Rom 5:5
1 Jn 3:24

4:9
1 Jn 2:20, 27

4:10
1 Thes 3:12
2 Thes 3:4

³God's will is for you to be holy, so stay away from all sexual sin. ⁴Then each of you will control his own body* and live in holiness and honor—⁵not in lustful passion like the pagans who do not know God and his ways. ⁶Never harm or cheat a Christian brother in this matter by violating his wife,* for the Lord avenges all such sins, as we have solemnly warned you before. ⁷God has called us to live holy lives, not impure lives. ⁸Therefore, anyone who refuses to live by these rules is not disobeying human teaching but is rejecting God, who gives his Holy Spirit to you.

⁹But we don't need to write to you about the importance of loving each other,* for God himself has taught you to love one another. ¹⁰Indeed, you already show your love for all the believers* throughout Macedonia. Even so, dear brothers and sisters, we urge you to love them even more.

4:4 Or *will know how to take a wife for himself;* or *will learn to live with his own wife;* Greek reads *will know how to possess his own vessel.* **4:6** Greek *Never harm or cheat a brother in this matter.* **4:9** Greek *about brotherly love.* **4:10** Greek *the brothers.*

CHECKLIST FOR ENCOURAGERS	Reference	Example	Suggested Application
The command to "encourage" others is found throughout the Bible. In 5:11-23, Paul gives many specific examples of how we can encourage others.	5:11	Build each other up.	Point out to someone a quality you appreciate in him or her.
	5:12	Honor leaders.	Look for ways to cooperate.
	5:13	Show leaders great respect.	Hold back your next critical comments about those in positions of responsibility. Say "thank you" to your leaders for their efforts.
	5:13	Live in peace.	Search for ways to get along with others.
	5:14	Warn the lazy.	Challenge someone to join you in a project.
	5:14	Encourage the timid.	Encourage those who are timid by reminding them of God's promises.
	5:14	Help the weak.	Support those who are weak by loving them and praying for them.
	5:14	Be patient.	Think of a situation that tries your patience, and plan ahead of time how you can stay calm.
	5:15	Resist revenge.	Instead of planning to get even with those who mistreat you, do good to them.
	5:16	Be joyful.	Remember that even in the midst of turmoil, God is in control.
	5:17	Pray continually.	God is always with you—talk to him.
	5:18	Give thanks.	Make a list of all the gifts God has given you, giving thanks to God for each one.
	5:19	Do not stifle the Holy Spirit.	Cooperate with the Spirit the next time he prompts you to participate in a Christian meeting.
	5:20	Do not scoff at prophecies.	Receive God's word from those who speak for him.
	5:22	Avoid every kind of evil.	Avoid situations where you will be drawn into temptation.
	5:23	Count on God's constant help.	Realize that the Christian life is to be lived not in our own strength but through God's power.

and wife. Therefore, the sexual experience must be limited to the marriage. Besides the physical consequences of sexual sin, there are also spiritual consequences. For more on why sexual sin is so harmful, see the note on 1 Corinthians 6:18.

• **4:3** It is God's will for you to be holy, but how can you go about doing that? The Bible teaches that holiness is not a state of being that you must manufacture on your own with hard work and good deeds and constant fear of failure. Instead, being made holy occurs in the process of living the Christian life. If you have accepted Christ's sacrifice on your behalf, then you are considered holy and complete in God's eyes. Yet you must continue to learn and grow during your time on earth. The Holy Spirit works in you, conforming you to the image of Christ (Romans 8:29).

4:4, 5 Paul said that lustful passions should not control God's people. Some argue that if they've already sinned by having lustful thoughts, they might as well go ahead with lustful actions too. Acting out sinful desires is harmful in several ways: (1) It causes people to excuse sin rather than to stop sinning; (2) it destroys marriages; (3) it is deliberate rebellion against God's Word; and (4) it always hurts someone else in addition to the sinner. Sinful action is more dangerous than sinful desire, so desires should not be acted out. Nevertheless, sinful desire is just as damaging to righteousness. Left unchecked, wrong desires will result in wrong actions and will turn people away from God.

¹¹Make it your goal to live a quiet life, minding your own business and working with your hands, just as we instructed you before. ¹²Then people who are not Christians will respect the way you live, and you will not need to depend on others.

The Hope of the Resurrection

¹³And now, dear brothers and sisters, we want you to know what will happen to the believers who have died* so you will not grieve like people who have no hope. ¹⁴For since we believe that Jesus died and was raised to life again, we also believe that when Jesus returns, God will bring back with him the believers who have died.

¹⁵We tell you this directly from the Lord: We who are still living when the Lord returns will not meet him ahead of those who have died.* ¹⁶For the Lord himself will come down from heaven with a commanding shout, with the voice of the archangel, and with the trumpet call of God. First, the Christians who have died* will rise from their graves. ¹⁷Then, together with them, we who are still alive and remain on the earth will be caught up in the clouds to meet the Lord in the air. Then we will be with the Lord forever. ¹⁸So encourage each other with these words.

5 Now concerning how and when all this will happen, dear brothers and sisters,* we don't really need to write you. ²For you know quite well that the day of the Lord's return will come unexpectedly, like a thief in the night. ³When people are saying, "Everything is peaceful and secure," then disaster will fall on them as suddenly as a pregnant woman's labor pains begin. And there will be no escape.

⁴But you aren't in the dark about these things, dear brothers and sisters, and you won't be surprised when the day of the Lord comes like a thief.* ⁵For you are all children of the light and of the day; we don't belong to darkness and night. ⁶So be on your guard, not asleep like the others. Stay alert and be clearheaded. ⁷Night is the time when people sleep and drinkers get drunk. ⁸But let us who live in the light be clearheaded, protected by the armor of faith and love, and wearing as our helmet the confidence of our salvation.

⁹For God chose to save us through our Lord Jesus Christ, not to pour out his anger on us. ¹⁰Christ died for us so that, whether we are dead or alive when he returns, we can live with him forever. ¹¹So encourage each other and build each other up, just as you are already doing.

4:11 Eph 4:28
2 Thes 3:10-12

4:14 Rom 14:9
1 Cor 15:3-4, 12

4:15 1 Cor 7:10, 25;
15:52

4:16 Matt 24:30
1 Cor 15:52
1 Thes 1:10
2 Thes 1:7

4:17 Acts 1:9
Rev 11:12

5:2 Matt 24:42-44

5:3 Jer 4:10; 6:14
Matt 24:39

5:4 1 Jn 2:8

5:5 John 12:36
Eph 5:9

5:7 Acts 2:15

5:8 Isa 59:17
Eph 6:14, 17
1 Pet 1:13

5:9 1 Thes 1:10
2 Thes 2:13-14

5:10 Rom 14:8-9

4:13 Greek *those who have fallen asleep;* also in 4:14. **4:15** Greek *those who have fallen asleep.* **4:16** Greek *the dead in Christ.* **5:1** Greek *brothers;* also in 5:4, 12, 14, 25, 26, 27. **5:4** Some manuscripts read *comes upon you as if you were thieves.*

4:11, 12 Christian living is more than simply loving other Christians. We must be responsible in all areas of life. Some of the Thessalonian Christians had adopted a life of idleness, depending on others for handouts. Some Greeks looked down on manual labor. So Paul told the Thessalonians to work hard and live quiet lives. You can't be effective in sharing your faith with others if they don't respect you. Whatever you do, do it faithfully and be a positive force in society.

• **4:13ff** The Thessalonians were wondering why many of their fellow believers had died and what would happen to them when Christ returned. Paul wanted the Thessalonians to understand that death is not the end of the story. The great hope for all believers is in the Resurrection. Because Jesus Christ came back to life, so will all believers, including those who have already died. Therefore, we need not despair when loved ones die or world events take a tragic turn. God will turn tragedy to triumph, poverty to riches, pain to glory, and defeat to victory. All believers throughout history will stand reunited in God's very presence, safe and secure. As Paul comforted the Thessalonians with the promise of the Resurrection, so we should comfort and reassure each other with this great hope.

4:15 What did Paul mean when he wrote, "We tell you this directly from the Lord"? Either this was something that the Lord had revealed directly to Paul, or it was a teaching of Jesus that had been passed along orally by the apostles and other Christians.

4:15-18 Knowing exactly *when* the dead will be raised, in relation to the other events at the Second Coming, is not as important as knowing why Paul wrote these words: to challenge believers to comfort and encourage one another. This passage can be a great comfort when any believer dies. The same love that should unite believers in this life (4:9) will unite believers when Christ returns and reigns for eternity.

4:16 An "archangel" is an angel with a position of authority and leadership. Michael is the only archangel mentioned in the New Testament (see Jude 1:9; Daniel 10:13; 12:1).

• **5:1-3** "How and when all this will happen" refers to the knowledge of what will happen in the future, specifically at the return of Christ. Efforts to determine the date of Christ's return are foolish. Don't be misled by anyone who claims to know. We are told here that no one knows and that even believers will be surprised. The Lord will return suddenly and unexpectedly, warns Paul, so be ready! Because no one knows when Jesus will come back to earth, we should be prepared at all times. Suppose he were to return today. How would he find you living? Are you ready to meet him? Live each day prepared to welcome Christ.

• **5:2** The "day of the Lord's return" is a future time when God will intervene directly and dramatically in world affairs. Predicted and discussed often in the Old Testament (Isaiah 13:6-12; Joel 2:28-32; Zephaniah 1:14-18), the day of the Lord will include both punishment and blessing. Christ will judge sin and set up his eternal Kingdom.

5:4, 5 It is good that we don't know exactly when Christ will return. If we knew the precise date, we might be tempted to be lazy in our work for Christ. Worse yet, we might plan to keep sinning and then turn to God right at the end. Heaven is not our only goal; we have work to do here. Christians must keep on doing God's work until death or until we see the unmistakable return of our Savior.

5:8 For more about the Christian's armor, see Ephesians 6:13-17.

5:9-11 As you near the end of a long race, your legs ache, your throat burns, and your whole body cries out for you to stop. This is when friends and fans are most valuable. Their encouragement helps you push through the pain to the finish line. In the same way,

5:12
1 Tim 5:17
5:15
Prov 20:22
Rom 12:17
1 Pet 3:9
5:16
Phil 4:4
5:17
Luke 18:1
5:18
Eph 5:20
5:19
Eph 4:30
5:20
1 Cor 14:1, 39

Paul's Final Advice

12Dear brothers and sisters, honor those who are your leaders in the Lord's work. They work hard among you and give you spiritual guidance. 13Show them great respect and whole-hearted love because of their work. And live peacefully with each other.

14Brothers and sisters, we urge you to warn those who are lazy. Encourage those who are timid. Take tender care of those who are weak. Be patient with everyone.

15See that no one pays back evil for evil, but always try to do good to each other and to all people.

16Always be joyful. 17Never stop praying. 18Be thankful in all circumstances, for this is God's will for you who belong to Christ Jesus.

19Do not stifle the Holy Spirit. 20Do not scoff at prophecies, 21but test everything that is said. Hold on to what is good. 22Stay away from every kind of evil.

Paul's Final Greetings

5:23
Rom 15:33
5:24
1 Cor 1:9

23Now may the God of peace make you holy in every way, and may your whole spirit and soul and body be kept blameless until our Lord Jesus Christ comes again. 24God will make this happen, for he who calls you is faithful.

25Dear brothers and sisters, pray for us.

26Greet all the brothers and sisters with Christian love.*

5:27
Col 4:16
5:28
Rom 16:20

27I command you in the name of the Lord to read this letter to all the brothers and sisters.

28May the grace of our Lord Jesus Christ be with you.

5:26 Greek *with a holy kiss.*

Christians are to encourage one another. Be sensitive to others' need for encouragement, and offer supportive words or actions.

5:12, 13 "Those who are your leaders in the Lord's work" probably refers to elders and deacons in the church. How can you honor your pastor and other church leaders? Express your appreciation, tell them how you have been helped by their leadership and teaching, and thank them for their ministry in your life. If you say nothing, how will they know where you stand? Remember, they need and deserve your support and love.

● **5:14** Don't loaf around with the lazy; warn them. Don't yell at the timid and weak; encourage and help them. At times it can be difficult to distinguish between idleness and timidity. Two people may be doing nothing—one out of laziness and the other out of shyness or fear of doing something wrong. The key to ministry is sensitivity: sensing the condition of each person and offering the appropriate remedy for each situation. You can't effectively help until you know the problem. You can't apply the medicine until you know where the wound is.

5:16-18 Our joy, prayers, and thankfulness should not fluctuate with our circumstances or feelings. Obeying these three commands—be joyful, never stop praying, and be thankful—often goes against our natural inclinations. When we make a conscious decision to do what God says, however, we will begin to see people in a new perspective. When we do God's will, we will find it easier to be joyful and thankful.

● **5:17** We cannot spend all our time on our knees, but it is possible to have a prayerful attitude at all times. This attitude is built upon acknowledging our dependence on God, realizing his presence within us, and determining to obey him fully. Then we will find it natural to pray frequent, spontaneous, short prayers. A prayerful attitude is not a substitute for regular times of prayer but should be an outgrowth of those times.

5:17 Have you ever grown tired of praying for something or someone? Paul said that believers should never stop praying. A Christian's persistence is an expression of faith that God answers prayer. Faith shouldn't die if the answers come slowly, for the delay may be God's way of working his will. When you feel tired of praying, know that God is present, always listening, always answering—in ways that he knows are best.

● **5:18** Paul was not teaching that we should thank God *for* everything that happens to us, but *in* everything. Evil does not come from God, so we should not thank him for it. But when evil strikes, we can still be thankful for God's presence and for the good that he will accomplish through the distress.

● **5:19** By warning us not to "stifle the Holy Spirit," Paul means that we should not ignore or toss aside the gifts the Holy Spirit gives. Here, he mentions prophecy (5:20); in 1 Corinthians 14:39, he mentions speaking in tongues. Sometimes spiritual gifts are controversial, and they may cause division in a church. Rather than trying to solve the problems, some Christians prefer to smother the gifts. This impoverishes the church. We should not stifle the Holy Spirit's work in anyone's life but encourage the full expression of these gifts to benefit the whole body of Christ.

5:20, 21 We shouldn't make fun of those who are called to speak for God ("scoff at prophecies"), but we should always "test everything that is said," checking their words against the Bible. We are on dangerous ground if we laugh at a person who speaks the truth. Instead, we should carefully check out what people say, accepting what is true and rejecting what is false.

5:22-24 Christians cannot avoid every kind of evil because we live in a sinful world. We can, however, make sure that we don't give evil a foothold by avoiding tempting situations and concentrating on obeying God.

5:23 The spirit, soul, and body refer not so much to the distinct parts of a person as to the entire being of a person. This expression is Paul's way of saying that God must be involved in *every* aspect of life. It is wrong to think that we can separate the spiritual life from everything else, obeying God only in some ethereal sense or living for him only one day each week. Christ must control *all* of us, not just a "religious" part.

5:27 For all the Christians to hear this letter, it had to be read in a public meeting—there were not enough copies to circulate. Paul wanted to make sure that everyone had the opportunity to hear his message because he was answering important questions and offering needed encouragement.

● **5:28** The Thessalonian church was young, and they needed help and encouragement. Both the persecution they faced and the temptations of their pagan culture were potential problems for these new Christians. Paul wrote to strengthen their faith and bolster their resistance to persecution and temptation. We, too, have a responsibility to help new believers—to make sure that they continue in their faith and don't become sidetracked by wrong beliefs or practices. First Thessalonians can better equip us to help our brothers and sisters in Christ.

"BUT I thought he said . . . ," "I'm sure he meant . . . ," "It is clear to me that we should . . . ," "I disagree. I think we must . . ."

Effective communication is difficult; often the message sent is *not* the message received in the home, marketplace, neighborhood, or church. Even when clearly stated or written, words can be misinterpreted and misunderstood, especially when filtered through the sieve of prejudices and preconceptions.

Paul faced this problem with the Thessalonians. He had written them earlier to help them grow in the faith, comforting and encouraging them by affirming the reality of Christ's return. Just a few months later, however, word came from Thessalonica that some had misunderstood Paul's teaching about the Second Coming. His announcement that Christ could come at any moment had caused some to stop working and just wait, rationalizing their idleness by pointing to Paul's teaching. Adding fuel to this fire was the continued persecution of the church. Many felt that indeed this must be the "day of the Lord."

Responding quickly, Paul sent a second letter to this young church. In it he gave further instruction concerning the Second Coming and the day of the Lord (2:1, 2). Second Thessalonians, therefore, continues the subject of 1 Thessalonians and is a call to continued courage and consistent conduct.

The letter begins with Paul's trademark—a personal greeting and a statement of thanksgiving for their faith (1:1–3). He mentions their perseverance in spite of their persecution and trials (1:4) and uses this situation to broach the subject of Christ's return. At that time, Christ will vindicate the righteous who endure and will punish the wicked (1:5–12).

Paul then directly answers the misunderstanding concerning the timing of the events of the end times. He tells them not to listen to rumors and reports that the day of the Lord has already begun (2:1, 2) because a number of events must occur before Christ returns (2:3–12). Meanwhile, they should stand firm for Christ's truth (2:13–15), receive God's encouragement and hope (2:16, 17), pray for strength and for the spread of the Lord's message (3:1–5), and warn those who are idle (3:6–15). Paul ends with personal greetings and a benediction (3:16–18).

Almost 2,000 years later, we stand much closer to the time of Christ's return; but we also would be wrong to see his imminent appearance as an excuse for idle waiting and heavenward gazing. Being prepared for his coming means spreading the gospel, reaching out to those in need, and building the church, his body. As you read 2 Thessalonians, then, see clearly the reality of his return and your responsibility to live for him until that day.

THE BLUEPRINT

1. The bright hope of Christ's return (1:1—2:17)
2. Living in the light of Christ's return (3:1–18)

Paul wrote to encourage those who were facing persecution and to correct a misunderstanding about the timing of Christ's return. The teaching about the Lord's return promoted idleness in this young church. The imminent coming of Christ should never make us idle; we should be even more busy—living purely, using our time well, and working for his Kingdom. We must work not only during easy times when it is convenient but also during difficult times. Christians must patiently watch for Christ's return and work for him while they wait.

MEGATHEMES

THEME	EXPLANATION	IMPORTANCE
Persecution	Paul encouraged the church to persevere in spite of troubles and trials. God will bring victory to his faithful followers and judge those who persecute them.	God promises to reward our faith by giving us his power and helping us bear persecution. Suffering for our faith will strengthen us to serve Christ. We must be faithful to him.
Christ's Return	Since Paul had said that the Lord could come at any moment, some of the Thessalonian believers had stopped working in order to wait for Christ.	Christ will return and bring total victory to all who trust in him. If we are ready, we need not be concerned about *when* he will return. We should stand firm, keep working, and wait for Christ.
Great Rebellion	Before Christ's return, there will be a great rebellion against God led by the man of lawlessness (the Antichrist). God will remove all the restraints on evil before he brings judgment on the rebels. The Antichrist will attempt to deceive many.	We should not be afraid when we see evil increase. God is in control, no matter how evil the world becomes. God guards us during Satan's attacks. We can have victory over evil by remaining faithful to God.
Persistence	Because church members had quit working and become disorderly and disobedient, Paul chastised them for their idleness. He called on them to show courage and true Christian conduct.	We must never get so tired of doing right that we quit. We can be persistent by making the most of our time and talents. Our endurance will be rewarded.

1. The bright hope of Christ's return
Greetings from Paul

1:1
1 Thes 1:1

1 This letter is from Paul, Silas,* and Timothy.

We are writing to the church in Thessalonica, to you who belong to God our Father and the Lord Jesus Christ.

1:2
Rom 1:7

²May God our Father* and the Lord Jesus Christ give you grace and peace.

1:1 Greek *Silvanus*, the Greek form of the name.   **1:2** Some manuscripts read *God the Father*.

● **1:1** Paul wrote this letter from Corinth less than a year after he had written 1 Thessalonians. He and his companions, Timothy and Silas, had visited Thessalonica on Paul's second missionary journey (Acts 17:1-10). They established the church there, but Paul had to leave suddenly because of persecution. This prompted him to write his first letter (1 Thessalonians), which contains words of comfort and encouragement. Paul then heard how the Thessalonians had responded to this letter. The good news was that they were continuing to grow in their faith. But the bad news was that false teachings about Christ's return were spreading, leading many to quit their jobs and wait for the end of the world. So Paul wrote to them again. While the purpose of Paul's first letter was to comfort the Thessalonians with the assurance of Christ's second coming, the purpose of his second letter is to correct false teaching about the Second Coming.

1:1 Paul, Silas, and Timothy were together in Corinth (Acts 18:5).

Paul wrote this letter on behalf of all three of them. Paul often included Timothy as a co-sender of his letters (see Philippians 1:1; Colossians 1:1; 1 Thessalonians 1:1). For more information about Paul, see his Profile in Acts 9, p. 1837. Silas's Profile is in Acts 16, p. 1859, and Timothy's Profile is found in 1 Timothy 2, p. 2059.

● **1:1** Thessalonica was the capital and largest city of the Roman province of Macedonia. The most important Roman highway—extending from Rome to the Orient—went through Thessalonica. This highway, along with the city's thriving seaport, made Thessalonica one of the wealthiest and most flourishing trade centers in the Roman Empire. Recognized as a free city, Thessalonica was allowed self-rule and was exempt from most of the restrictions placed by Rome on other cities. Because of this open climate, however, the city had many pagan religions and cultural influences that challenged the Christians' faith.

Encouragement during Persecution

3Dear brothers and sisters,* we can't help but thank God for you, because your faith is flourishing and your love for one another is growing. 4We proudly tell God's other churches about your endurance and faithfulness in all the persecutions and hardships you are suffering. 5And God will use this persecution to show his justice and to make you worthy of his Kingdom, for which you are suffering. 6In his justice he will pay back those who persecute you.

7And God will provide rest for you who are being persecuted and also for us when the Lord Jesus appears from heaven. He will come with his mighty angels, 8in flaming fire, bringing judgment on those who don't know God and on those who refuse to obey the Good News of our Lord Jesus. 9They will be punished with eternal destruction, forever separated from the Lord and from his glorious power. 10When he comes on that day, he will receive glory from his holy people—praise from all who believe. And this includes you, for you believed what we told you about him.

11So we keep on praying for you, asking our God to enable you to live a life worthy of his call. May he give you the power to accomplish all the good things your faith prompts you to do. 12Then the name of our Lord Jesus will be honored because of the way you live, and you will be honored along with him. This is all made possible because of the grace of our God and Lord, Jesus Christ.*

1:5
Phil 1:28
1 Thes 2:12
1:6
Rev 6:10
1:7
Matt 25:31
1 Thes 4:16
1:8
Ps 79:6
Isa 66:15
1:9
Isa 2:10, 19, 21
1 Thes 5:3
2 Thes 2:8
1:10
John 17:10
1 Thes 3:13
1:12
Isa 66:5
Mal 1:11

Events prior to the Lord's Second Coming

2 Now, dear brothers and sisters,* let us clarify some things about the coming of our Lord Jesus Christ and how we will be gathered to meet him. 2Don't be so easily shaken or alarmed by those who say that the day of the Lord has already begun. Don't believe them, even if they claim to have had a spiritual vision, a revelation, or a letter supposedly from us.

2:1
1 Thes 4:13-17
2:2
2 Thes 2:15; 3:17

1:3 Greek *Brothers.*   1:12 Or *of our God and our Lord Jesus Christ.*   2:1 Greek *brothers;* also in 2:13, 15.

1:3ff Regardless of the contents of Paul's letters, his style was affirming. Paul began most of his letters by stating what he most appreciated about his readers and the joy he felt because of their faith in God. We also should look for ways to encourage and build up other believers. For more on encouragement, see the note in 1 Timothy 4:12-16.

• **1:4** The keys to surviving persecution and trials are endurance and faithfulness. When faced with crushing troubles, we can have faith that God is using our trials for our good and for his glory. Knowing that God is fair and just will give us patience in our suffering because we know that he has not forgotten us. In God's perfect timing, he will relieve our suffering and punish those who persecute us. Do you trust God's timing? That is the first step toward growing in endurance and faithfulness.

• **1:4-6** Paul had been persecuted during his first visit to Thessalonica (Acts 17:5-9). No doubt those who had responded to his message and had become Christians were continuing to be persecuted by both Jews and Gentiles. In Paul's first letter to the Thessalonians, he had said that Christ's return would bring deliverance from persecution for the believers and judgment on the persecutors. But this caused the people to expect Christ's return right away to rescue and vindicate them. So Paul had to point out that while waiting for God's Kingdom, believers could and should grow in their endurance and faithfulness through the hardships they were suffering.

• **1:5** As we live for Christ, we will experience troubles because we are trying to be God's people in a perverse world. Some people say that troubles are the result of sin or lack of faith, but Paul teaches that they may be a part of God's plan for believers. Our problems can help us look upward and forward, instead of inward (Mark 13:35, 36; Philippians 3:13, 14), they can build strong character (Romans 5:3, 4), and they can provide us with opportunities to comfort others who also are struggling (2 Corinthians 1:3-5). Your troubles may be an indication that you are taking a stand for Christ. When you do so, you are experiencing the privilege of showing that you are worthy of God's Kingdom (see also 1:11).

• **1:7** The "rest" mentioned by Paul has two dimensions. We can rest in knowing that our sufferings are strengthening us, making us ready for Christ's Kingdom. We can also rest in the fact that one day everyone will stand before God. At that time, wrongs will be righted, judgment will be pronounced, and evil will be terminated.

1:9 The "eternal destruction" that Paul describes is the lake of fire (see Revelation 20:14)—the place of eternal separation from God. Those people who will be separated from God in eternity will no longer have any hope for salvation.

1:11, 12 As Christians, our calling from God is to become like Christ (Romans 8:29). This is a gradual, lifelong process that will be completed when we see Christ face to face (1 John 3:2). To be "worthy" of this calling means to *want* to do what is right and good (as Christ would). We aren't perfect yet, but we're moving in that direction as God works in us.

2:1ff Paul describes the end of the world and Christ's second coming. He says that great suffering and trouble lie ahead, but evil will not prevail because Christ will return to judge all people. Although Paul presents a few signs of the end times, his emphasis, like Jesus' (Mark 13), is the need for each person to prepare for Christ's return by living rightly day by day. If we are ready, we won't have to be concerned about the preceding events or the timing of Christ's return. God controls all events. (See 1 Thessalonians 4 and 5 for Paul's earlier teaching on this subject.)

2:1, 2 In the Bible, "the day of the Lord" is used in two ways: It can mean the end times (beginning with Christ's birth and continuing until today), and it can mean the final judgment day (in the future). Because some false teachers were saying that judgment day had come, many believers were waiting expectantly for their vindication and for relief from suffering. But judgment day had not yet come; other events would have to happen first.

• **2:2** "A spiritual vision, a revelation, or a letter" could refer to the fact that false teaching had come from (1) someone claiming to have had a divine revelation, (2) someone passing on a teaching as though it were from Paul, or (3) someone distributing a letter supposedly written by Paul.

2:3
1 Tim 4:1

2:4
Isa 14:13-14
1 Cor 8:5

2:7
1 Jn 4:3

2:8
Job 4:9
Isa 11:4
Rev 19:15

³Don't be fooled by what they say. For that day will not come until there is a great rebellion against God and the man of lawlessness* is revealed—the one who brings destruction.* ⁴He will exalt himself and defy everything that people call god and every object of worship. He will even sit in the temple of God, claiming that he himself is God.

⁵Don't you remember that I told you about all this when I was with you? ⁶And you know what is holding him back, for he can be revealed only when his time comes. ⁷For this lawlessness is already at work secretly, and it will remain secret until the one who is holding it back steps out of the way. ⁸Then the man of lawlessness will be revealed, but the Lord Jesus will kill him with the breath of his mouth and destroy him by the splendor of his coming.

2:3a Some manuscripts read *the man of sin.*   **2:3b** Greek *the son of destruction.*

LOCATION OF THESSA-LONICA

After Paul visited Thessalonica on his second missionary journey, he went on to Berea, Athens, and Corinth (Acts 17—18). From Corinth, Paul wrote his two letters to the Thessalonian church.

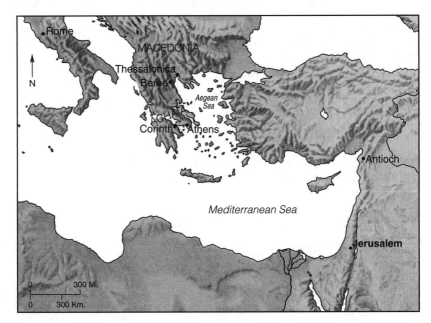

2:3 Throughout history there have been individuals who epitomized evil and who were hostile to everything Christ stands for (see 1 John 2:18; 4:3; 2 John 1:7). These antichrists have lived in every generation and will continue to work their evil. Then just before Christ's second coming, "the man of lawlessness . . . the one who brings destruction," a completely evil man, will arise. He will be Satan's tool, equipped with Satan's power (2:9). This lawless man will be *the* Antichrist.

It is dangerous, however, to label any person as the Antichrist and to try to predict Christ's coming based on that assumption. Paul mentions a man of lawlessness, not so we might attempt to identify him, but so we might be ready for anything that threatens our faith. If our faith is strong, we don't need to be afraid of what lies ahead, because we know that this lawless man has already been defeated by God, no matter how powerful he becomes or how terrible our situation seems. God is in control, and he will be victorious. Our task is to be prepared for Christ's return and to spread the Good News so that even more people will also be prepared.

● **2:3ff** When Paul first wrote to the Thessalonians, they were in danger of losing hope in the Second Coming. Then they shifted to the opposite extreme—some of them thought that Jesus would be coming at any minute and so they stopped being productive for God. Paul tried to restore the balance by describing certain events that would happen before Christ's return.

2:6, 7 What holds back the lawless one? We do not know for certain. Three possibilities have been suggested: (1) government and law, which help to curb evil; (2) the ministry and activity of the church and the effects of the Good News; or (3) the Holy Spirit. The Bible is not clear on who this restrainer is, only that he will not restrain forever. But we should not fear this time when the restraint is removed—God is far stronger than the man of lawlessness, and God will save his people.

2:7 "This lawlessness is already at work secretly" means that the work that this Antichrist will do is already going on. *Secretly* means something no one can discover but something God will reveal. *Lawlessness* is the hidden, subtle, underlying force from which all sin springs. Civilization still has a veneer of decency through law enforcement, education, science, and reason. Although we are horrified by criminal acts, we have yet to see the real horror of complete lawlessness. This will happen when "the one who is holding it back steps out of the way." Why will God allow this to happen? To show people and nations their own sinfulness, and to show them by bitter experience the true alternative to the lordship of Christ. People totally without God can act no better than vicious animals. Lawlessness, to a certain extent, is already going on, but the man of lawlessness has not yet been revealed.

9This man will come to do the work of Satan with counterfeit power and signs and miracles. 10He will use every kind of evil deception to fool those on their way to destruction, because they refuse to love and accept the truth that would save them. 11So God will cause them to be greatly deceived, and they will believe these lies. 12Then they will be condemned for enjoying evil rather than believing the truth.

Believers Should Stand Firm

13As for us, we can't help but thank God for you, dear brothers and sisters loved by the Lord. We are always thankful that God chose you to be among the first* to experience salvation—a salvation that came through the Spirit who makes you holy and through your belief in the truth. 14He called you to salvation when we told you the Good News; now you can share in the glory of our Lord Jesus Christ.

15With all these things in mind, dear brothers and sisters, stand firm and keep a strong grip on the teaching we passed on to you both in person and by letter.

16Now may our Lord Jesus Christ himself and God our Father, who loved us and by his grace gave us eternal comfort and a wonderful hope, 17comfort you and strengthen you in every good thing you do and say.

2. Living in the light of Christ's return
Paul's Request for Prayer

3 Finally, dear brothers and sisters,* we ask you to pray for us. Pray that the Lord's message will spread rapidly and be honored wherever it goes, just as when it came to you. 2Pray, too, that we will be rescued from wicked and evil people, for not everyone is a believer. 3But the Lord is faithful; he will strengthen you and guard you from the evil one.* 4And we are confident in the Lord that you are doing and will continue to do the things we commanded you. 5May the Lord lead your hearts into a full understanding and expression of the love of God and the patient endurance that comes from Christ.

2:9 Matt 24:24; Rev 13:13
2:10 1 Cor 1:18
2:11 Rom 1:24, 28; 2 Tim 4:4
2:12 Rom 1:18, 32; 2:8
2:13 Deut 33:12; Eph 1:4
2:14 1 Thes 4:7; 5:9
2:15 1 Cor 11:2; 16:13
2:16 John 3:16
2:17 1 Thes 3:2; 5:11
3:1 1 Thes 1:8; 5:25
3:2 Rom 15:31
3:3 1 Cor 1:9
3:4 1 Thes 4:10
3:5 1 Chr 29:18

2:13 Some manuscripts read *chose you from the very beginning.*   **3:1** Greek *brothers;* also in 3:6, 13.
3:3 Or *from evil.*

2:9 This evil man will use "counterfeit power and signs and miracles" to deceive and draw a following. Miracles from God can help strengthen our faith and lead people to Christ, but all miracles are not necessarily from God. Christ's miracles were significant, not just because of their power, but because of their purpose—to help, to heal, and to point us to God. The man of lawlessness will have power to do amazing things, but his power will be from Satan. He will use this power to destroy and to lead people away from God and toward himself. If any so-called religious personality draws attention only to himself or herself, his or her work is not from God.

• **2:10-12** Does God cause people to be deceived? To understand God's allowing such deception, we must first understand God's nature. (1) God himself is good (Psalm 11:7). (2) God created a good world that fell because of humanity's sin (Romans 5:12). (3) Someday God will re-create the world and it will be good again (Revelation 21:1). (4) God is stronger than evil (Matthew 13:41-43; Revelation 19:11-21). (5) God allows evil and thus has control over it. God did not create evil, and he offers help to those who wish to overcome it (Matthew 11:28-30). (6) God uses everything—both good and evil—for his good purposes (Genesis 50:20; Romans 8:28).

The Bible reveals a God who hates all evil and will one day do away with it completely and forever (Revelation 20:10-15). God does not entice anyone to become evil. Those committed to evil, however, may be used by God to sin even more in order to hasten their deserved judgment (see Exodus 11:10). We don't need to understand every detail of how God works in order to have perfect confidence in his absolute power over evil and his total goodness toward us.

2:13 Paul consistently taught that salvation begins and ends with God. We can do nothing to be saved on our own merit—we must accept God's gift of salvation (see the note on Ephesians 1:4). There is no other way to receive forgiveness from sin. Paul is encouraging the Thessalonian believers by reminding them that they were chosen by God from the beginning. Being made holy is the process of Christian growth through which the Holy Spirit makes us like Christ (Romans 8:29). See the note on 1:11, 12.

2:14 God worked through Paul and his companions to tell the Good News so that people could share in Christ's glory. It may seem strange that God works through us—fallible, unfaithful, untrustworthy human creatures. But he has given us the fantastic privilege of accomplishing his great mission—telling the world how to find salvation.

• **2:15** Paul knew that the Thessalonians would face pressure from persecutions, false teachers, worldliness, and apathy to waver from the truth and to leave the faith. So he urged them to "stand firm" and hold on to the truth they had been taught both through his letters and in person. We also may face persecution, false teachings, worldliness, and apathy. We should hold on to the truth of Christ's teachings because our life depends on it. Never forget the reality of Christ's life and love!

3:1-3 Beneath the surface of the routine of daily life, a fierce struggle among invisible spiritual powers is being waged. Our main defense is prayer that God will protect us from the evil one and that he will strengthen us. (See also comments on Ephesians 6:10-19 concerning our armor for spiritual warfare.) The following guidelines can help you prepare for and survive satanic attacks: (1) Take the threat of spiritual attack seriously; (2) pray for strength and help from God; (3) study the Bible to recognize Satan's style and tactics; (4) memorize Scripture so it will be a source of help no matter where you are; (5) associate with those who speak the truth; and (6) practice what you are taught by sound spiritual leaders.

An Exhortation to Proper Living

3:6
Rom 16:17
1 Cor 11:2

6And now, dear brothers and sisters, we give you this command in the name of our Lord Jesus Christ: Stay away from all believers* who live idle lives and don't follow the tradition they received* from us. 7For you know that you ought to imitate us. We were not idle when

3:8
Acts 18:3
1 Thes 2:9

we were with you. 8We never accepted food from anyone without paying for it. We worked hard day and night so we would not be a burden to any of you. 9We certainly had the right to

3:9
Matt 10:10
1 Cor 9:4, 6

ask you to feed us, but we wanted to give you an example to follow. 10Even while we were with you, we gave you this command: "Those unwilling to work will not get to eat."

3:10
1 Thes 4:11

11Yet we hear that some of you are living idle lives, refusing to work and meddling in other people's business. 12We command such people and urge them in the name of the Lord Jesus

3:11
1 Tim 5:13

Christ to settle down and work to earn their own living. 13As for the rest of you, dear brothers and sisters, never get tired of doing good.

3:12
1 Thes 4:11

14Take note of those who refuse to obey what we say in this letter. Stay away from them so

3:15
Gal 6:1
1 Thes 5:14

they will be ashamed. 15Don't think of them as enemies, but warn them as you would a brother or sister.*

Paul's Final Greetings

3:16
Rom 15:33

16Now may the Lord of peace himself give you his peace at all times and in every situation. The Lord be with you all.

3:17
1 Cor 16:21
Gal 6:11
Col 4:18
Phlm 1:19

17HERE IS MY GREETING IN MY OWN HANDWRITING—PAUL. I DO THIS IN ALL MY LETTERS TO PROVE THEY ARE FROM ME. 18May the grace of our Lord Jesus Christ be with you all.

3:6a Greek *from every brother.*   **3:6b** Some manuscripts read *you received.*   **3:15** Greek *as a brother.*

• **3:6-10** Paul was writing here about the person who is lazy. Paul explained that when he and his companions were in Thessalonica, they worked hard, buying what they needed rather than becoming a burden to any of the believers. The rule they followed was, "Those unwilling to work will not get to eat." There's a difference between leisure and laziness. Relaxation and recreation provide a necessary and much needed balance to our lives; when it is time to work, however, Christians should jump right in. We should make the most of our talent and time, doing all we can to provide for ourselves and our dependents. Rest when you should be resting, and work when you should be working.

• **3:6-15** Some people in the Thessalonian church were falsely teaching that because Christ would return any day, people should set aside their responsibilities, quit work, do no future planning, and just wait for the Lord. But their lack of activity only led them into sin. They became a burden to the church which was supporting them, they wasted time that could have been used for helping others, and they became meddlers (3:11). These church members may have thought that they were being more spiritual by not working, but Paul tells them to be responsible and get back to work. Being ready for Christ means obeying him in every area of life. Because we know that Christ is coming, we must live in such a way that our faith and our daily practice will please him when he arrives.

3:11, 12 An idle person who doesn't work ends up filling his or her time with less than helpful activities, like gossip. Rumors and hearsay are tantalizing, exciting to hear, and make us feel like insiders. But they tear people down. If you often find your nose in other people's business, you may be underemployed. Look for a task to do for Christ or for your family, and get to work.

• **3:14, 15** Paul counseled the church to stop supporting financially and associating with those who persisted in idleness. Hunger and loneliness can be very effective ways to make the idle person become productive. Paul was not advising coldness or cruelty, but tough love to help a person become responsible.

3:18 The book of 2 Thessalonians is especially meaningful for those who are being persecuted or are under pressure because of their faith. In chapter 1 we are told what suffering can do for us. In chapter 2 we are assured of final victory. In chapter 3 we are encouraged to continue living responsibly in spite of difficult circumstances. Christ's return is more than a doctrine; it is a promise. It is not just for the future; it has a vital impact on how we live now.

PHILEMON

AT THE foreman's signal, the giant ball is released, and with dynamite force and a reverberating crash, it meets the wall, snapping bricks like twigs and scattering pieces of mortar. Repeatedly, the powerful pendulum works, and soon the barrier has been reduced to rubble. Then it is carted away so that construction can begin.

Life has many walls and fences that divide, separate, and compartmentalize. Not made of wood or stone, they are personal obstructions, blocking people from each other and from God. But Christ came as the great wall remover, tearing down the sin partition that separates us from God and blasting the barriers that keep us from each other. His death and resurrection opened the way to eternal life to bring all who believe into the family of God (see Ephesians 2:14–18).

Roman, Greek, and Jewish cultures were littered with barriers, as society assigned people to classes and expected them to stay in their place—men and women, slave and free, rich and poor, Jews and Gentiles, Greeks and barbarians, pious and pagan. But with the message of Christ, the walls came down, and Paul could declare, "In this new life, it doesn't matter if you are a Jew or a Gentile, circumcised or uncircumcised, barbaric, uncivilized, slave, or free. Christ is all that matters, and he lives in all of us" (Colossians 3:11).

This life-changing truth forms the backdrop for the letter to Philemon. One of three personal letters in the Bible, the letter to Philemon is Paul's personal plea for a slave. Onesimus "belonged" to Philemon, a member of the Colossian church and Paul's friend. But Onesimus, the slave, had stolen from his master and had run away. He had run to Rome, where he had met Paul, and there he had responded to the Good News and had come to faith in Christ (1:10). So Paul wrote to Philemon and reintroduced Onesimus to him, explaining that he was sending him back, not just as a slave but as a brother (1:11, 12, 16). Tactfully he asked Philemon to accept and forgive his brother (1:10, 14, 15, 20). The barriers of the past and the new ones erected by Onesimus's desertion and theft should divide them no longer—they are one in Christ.

This small book is a masterpiece of grace and tact and a profound demonstration of the power of Christ and of true Christian fellowship in action. What barriers stand in your home, neighborhood, and church? What separates you from fellow believers? Race? Status? Wealth? Education? Personality? As with Philemon, God calls you to seek unity, breaking down those walls and embracing your brothers and sisters in Christ.

VITAL STATISTICS

PURPOSE:
To convince Philemon to forgive his runaway slave, Onesimus, and to accept him as a brother in the faith

AUTHOR:
Paul

ORIGINAL AUDIENCE:
Philemon, who was probably a wealthy member of the Colossian church

DATE WRITTEN:
Approximately A.D. 60, during Paul's first imprisonment in Rome, at about the same time Ephesians and Colossians were written

SETTING:
Slavery was very common in the Roman Empire, and evidently some Christians had slaves. Paul does not condemn the institution of slavery in his writings, but he makes a radical statement by calling this slave Philemon's brother in Christ.

KEY VERSES:
"It seems Onesimus ran away for a little while so that you could have him back forever. He is no longer like a slave to you. He is more than a slave, for he is a beloved brother, especially to me. Now he will mean much more to you, both as a man and as a brother in the Lord" (1:15, 16).

KEY PEOPLE:
Paul, Philemon, Onesimus

KEY PLACES:
Colosse, Rome

SPECIAL FEATURES:
This is a private, personal letter to a friend.

THE BLUEPRINT

1. Paul's appreciation of Philemon (1:1–7)
2. Paul's appeal for Onesimus (1:8–25)

Paul pleads on behalf of Onesimus, a runaway slave. Paul's intercession for him illustrates what Christ has done for us. As Paul interceded for a slave, so Christ intercedes for us, slaves to sin. As Onesimus was reconciled to Philemon, so we are reconciled to God through Christ. As Paul offered to pay the debts of a slave, so Christ paid our debt of sin. Like Onesimus, we must return to God our Master and serve him.

MEGATHEMES

THEME	EXPLANATION	IMPORTANCE
Forgiveness	Philemon was Paul's friend and the legal owner of the slave Onesimus. Paul asked Philemon not to punish Onesimus but to forgive and restore him as a new Christian brother.	Christian relationships must be full of forgiveness and acceptance. Can you forgive those who have wronged you?
Barriers	Slavery was widespread in the Roman Empire, but no one is lost to God or beyond his love. Slavery was a barrier between people, but Christian love and fellowship are to overcome such barriers.	In Christ we are one family. No walls of racial, economic, or political differences should separate us. Let Christ work through you to remove barriers between Christian brothers and sisters.
Respect	Paul was a friend of both Philemon and Onesimus. He had the authority as an apostle to tell Philemon what to do. Yet Paul chose to appeal to his friend in Christian love rather than to order him what to do.	Tactful persuasion accomplishes a great deal more than commands when dealing with people. Remember to exhibit courtesy and respect in your relationships.

1. Paul's appreciation of Philemon

Greetings from Paul

This letter is from Paul, a prisoner for preaching the Good News about Christ Jesus, and from our brother Timothy.

I am writing to Philemon, our beloved co-worker, ²and to our sister Apphia, and to our fellow soldier Archippus, and to the church that meets in your* house.

³May God our Father and the Lord Jesus Christ give you grace and peace.

1:1
Eph 4:1
Phil 1:7
Phlm 1:9, 23

1:2
Rom 16:5
Phil 2:25
Col 4:17

Paul's Thanksgiving and Prayer

⁴I always thank my God when I pray for you, Philemon, ⁵because I keep hearing about your faith in the Lord Jesus and your love for all of God's people. ⁶And I am praying that you will put into action the generosity that comes from your faith as you understand and experience

1:4
Rom 1:8-9
1:6
Phil 1:9

2 Throughout this letter, *you* and *your* are singular except in verses 3, 22, and 25.

●**1:1** Paul wrote this letter from Rome in about A.D. 60, when he was under house arrest (see Acts 28:30, 31). Onesimus was a domestic slave who belonged to Philemon, a wealthy man and a member of the church in Colosse. Onesimus had run away from Philemon and had made his way to Rome, where he met Paul, who apparently led him to Christ (1:10). Paul convinced Onesimus that running from his problems wouldn't solve them, and he persuaded Onesimus to return to his master. Paul wrote this letter to Philemon to ask him to be reconciled to his runaway slave.

1:1 For more information on Paul's life, see his Profile in Acts 9, p. 1837. Timothy's name is included with Paul's in 2 Corinthians, 1 Thessalonians, 2 Thessalonians, Philippians, Colossians, and Philemon—the last three of these letters are from a group known as the "Prison Letters." Timothy was one of Paul's trusted companions; Paul wrote two letters to him—1 and 2 Timothy. See Timothy's Profile in 1 Timothy 2, p. 2059.

1:1 Philemon was a Greek landowner living in Colosse. He had been converted under Paul's ministry, and the Colossian church met in his home. Onesimus was one of Philemon's slaves.

●**1:2** Apphia may have been Philemon's wife. Archippus may have been Philemon's son or perhaps an elder in the Colossian church. In either case, Paul included him as a recipient of the

letter, possibly so Archippus could read the letter with Philemon and encourage him to take Paul's advice.

1:2 The early churches often would meet in people's homes. Because of sporadic persecutions and the great expense involved, church buildings were typically not constructed at this time.

●**1:4-7** Like cold water on a long hike, this Christian brother Philemon knew how to be refreshing. He was able to revive and restore his brothers and sisters in the faith. His love and generosity had replenished and stimulated them. Philemon also encouraged Paul by his love and loyalty. Are you a refreshing influence on others, or do your attitude and temperament add to the burden they carry? Instead of draining others' energy and motivation with complaints and problems, replenish their spirits by encouragement, love, and a helpful attitude.

1:6 Paul's prayer for Philemon was setting the stage for the request Paul would make in this letter. Philemon was active in his faith and generous in sharing its blessings. As he gained fuller understanding of all that Christ had done on his behalf, this knowledge should cause him to respond appropriately to Paul's request regarding Onesimus. Are you active and effective in sharing with others your faith, your resources, and your love?

1:7
2 Cor 7:4, 13

all the good things we have in Christ. ⁷Your love has given me much joy and comfort, my brother, for your kindness has often refreshed the hearts of God's people.

2. Paul's appeal for Onesimus

⁸That is why I am boldly asking a favor of you. I could demand it in the name of Christ because it is the right thing for you to do. ⁹But because of our love, I prefer simply to ask you. Consider this as a request from me—Paul, an old man and now also a prisoner for the sake of Christ Jesus.*

1:9
Eph 3:1; 4:1
Phil 1:7

9 Or *a prisoner of Christ Jesus.*

ONESIMUS

God must have a special love for runaways. The pages of Scripture record dozens of people who were prone to flight. From Adam and Eve's attempt to elude God, through Jacob's escape from his brother, past generations of God's people on the run, to that inner circle of disciples who fled from the garden when Jesus was captured, the Bible is a collection of runaway lives. God's special love for runaways is beautifully illustrated in the life of a slave named Onesimus.

We are not told why Onesimus ran away from Philemon's house in Colosse. Eventually, he and Paul were reunited in Rome. Though we might crave details, Paul simply wrote that Onesimus became a follower of Jesus. Later, his spiritual growth caused Paul to call him a "faithful and beloved brother" (Colossians 4:9).

Eventually, Paul and Onesimus decided it was time for the runaway slave to return home. Paul wrote a letter of explanation to his friend Philemon, assuring him that Onesimus would now serve him wholeheartedly. Although the culture of the day gave masters complete control over their slaves and although severe punishment usually faced a runaway, Paul challenged Philemon to think of Onesimus more as a brother than as a slave. Paul took responsibility for any restitution Philemon might require of Onesimus. As difficult as it might be for him, Onesimus, the runaway slave turned believer, had to return and face his old life as a new person.

When God finds runaways, he often sends them back to the very places and people from which they ran in the first place. As God has become real in your life, how has your past come into new perspective? Are there still situations from your past that need to be resolved? In what ways has your relationship with Christ given you new opportunities and resources to face what you used to run away from?

Strengths and accomplishments	• Tracked down and listened to the apostle Paul's message • Grew into an able believer and assistant to Paul while in Rome • Returned to his previous master as a willing slave
Weakness and mistake	• Ran away from his master, Philemon
Lessons from his life	• God is in the radical forgiveness business • We cannot run from God and hope to escape
Vital statistics	• Where: Colosse • Occupation: Slave
Key verses	"It seems Onesimus ran away for a little while so that you could have him back forever. He is no longer like a slave to you. He is more than a slave, for he is a beloved brother, especially to me. Now he will mean much more to you, both as a man and as a brother in the Lord" (Philemon 1:15-16).

Onesimus is mentioned in Colossians 4:9 and is the subject of Paul's letter to Philemon.

1:8, 9 Because Paul was an elder and an apostle, he could have used his authority with Philemon, commanding him to deal kindly with his runaway slave. But Paul based his request not on his own authority but on Philemon's Christian commitment. Paul wanted Philemon's heartfelt, not grudging, obedience. When you know something is right and you have the power to demand it, do you appeal to your authority or to the other person's commitment?

Paul provides a good example of how to deal with conflict between Christians. When reconciling a separation or mediating a dispute, trust must be rebuilt between the conflicting parties. Notice the steps that Paul used to help rebuild the trust: (1) He identified with those involved, calling Philemon "brother" and Onesimus "my child." (2) He requested, not ordered, Philemon

to do the right thing. (3) He sought Philemon's voluntary consent, not his submission to rules or authority. (4) He appealed to Christian love, not to power or authority. (5) He agreed to absorb the loss and pay any cost for restoration. Instead of overusing power or position, use Paul's approach to rebuild a trusting relationship.

¹⁰I appeal to you to show kindness to my child, Onesimus. I became his father in the faith while here in prison. ¹¹Onesimus* hasn't been of much use to you in the past, but now he is very useful to both of us. ¹²I am sending him back to you, and with him comes my own heart.

¹³I wanted to keep him here with me while I am in these chains for preaching the Good News, and he would have helped me on your behalf. ¹⁴But I didn't want to do anything without your consent. I wanted you to help because you were willing, not because you were forced. ¹⁵It seems you lost Onesimus for a little while so that you could have him back forever. ¹⁶He is no longer like a slave to you. He is more than a slave, for he is a beloved brother, especially to me. Now he will mean much more to you, both as a man and as a brother in the Lord.

¹⁷So if you consider me your partner, welcome him as you would welcome me. ¹⁸If he has wronged you in any way or owes you anything, charge it to me. ¹⁹I, PAUL, WRITE THIS WITH MY OWN HAND: I WILL REPAY IT. AND I WON'T MENTION THAT YOU OWE ME YOUR VERY SOUL!

²⁰Yes, my brother, please do me this favor* for the Lord's sake. Give me this encouragement in Christ.

²¹I am confident as I write this letter that you will do what I ask and even more! ²²One more thing—please prepare a guest room for me, for I am hoping that God will answer your prayers and let me return to you soon.

Paul's Final Greetings

²³Epaphras, my fellow prisoner in Christ Jesus, sends you his greetings. ²⁴So do Mark, Aristarchus, Demas, and Luke, my co-workers.

²⁵May the grace of the Lord Jesus Christ be with your spirit.

11 *Onesimus* means "useful."   20 Greek *onaimen*, a play on the name Onesimus.

1:10
1 Cor 4:14
Col 4:9

1:13
Phil 2:30

1:14
2 Cor 9:7
1 Pet 5:2

1:15
Gen 45:5, 8

1:16
Matt 23:8
1 Cor 7:22
Eph 6:9

1:17
2 Cor 8:23

1:19
1 Cor 16:21

1:22
Phil 1:25-26; 2:24

1:23
Col 1:7; 4:10

1:25
Gal 6:18

1:10 A master had the legal right to kill a runaway slave, so Onesimus feared for his life. Paul wrote this letter to Philemon to help him understand his new relationship with Onesimus, who was now a Christian brother, not a mere possession.

- **1:10ff** From his prison cell, Paul had led Onesimus to the Lord. Paul asked Philemon to forgive his runaway slave who had become a Christian and, even going beyond forgiveness, to accept Onesimus as a brother. As Christians, we should forgive as we have been forgiven (Matthew 6:12; Ephesians 4:31, 32). True forgiveness means that we treat the one we've forgiven as we would want to be treated. Is there someone you say you have forgiven but who still needs your kindness?

- **1:11-15** *Onesimus* means "useful." Paul used a play on words, saying that Onesimus had not been much use to Philemon in the past but now had become very useful to both Philemon and Paul. Although Paul wanted to keep Onesimus with him, he was sending Onesimus back, requesting that Philemon accept him not only as a forgiven runaway servant but also as a brother in Christ.

1:15, 16 Slavery was widespread throughout the Roman Empire. In these early days, Christians did not have the political power to change the slavery system. Paul didn't condemn or condone slavery, but he worked to transform relationships. The Good News begins to change social structures by changing the *people* within those structures. (See also 1 Corinthians 7:20-24; Ephesians 6:5-9; Colossians 3:22–4:1 for more on master/slave relationships.)

- **1:16** What a difference Onesimus's status as a Christian made in his relationship to Philemon. He was no longer merely a slave, but he was also a brother. That meant that both Onesimus and Philemon were members of God's family—equals in Christ. A Christian's status as a member of God's family transcends all other distinctions among believers. Do you look down on any fellow Christians? Remember, they are your equals before Christ (Galatians 3:28). How you treat your brothers and sisters in Christ's family reflects your true Christian commitment.

1:17 Paul called Philemon his "partner," but he did not mean a partner in the business sense of the word. Philemon was a partner in grace. Paul and Philemon shared the same experience in Jesus Christ of being saved; in that sense, they were equals. Too often our relationships in the church don't possess true partnership but reflect merely tolerance of one another. Do you have room in your heart to welcome other believers warmly? Treat them as partners in God's grace and love, not just fellow workers. Let your common interests in Christ and your common feeling of gratitude for Christ's love knit you together with others.

1:17-19 Paul genuinely loved Onesimus. Paul showed his love by personally guaranteeing payment for any stolen goods or wrongs for which Onesimus might be responsible. Paul's investment in the life of this new believer certainly encouraged and strengthened Onesimus's faith. Are there young believers who need you to demonstrate such self-sacrifice toward them? Be grateful when you can invest in the lives of others, helping them with Bible study, prayer, encouragement, support, and friendship.

- **1:19** Philemon owed his soul to Paul, meaning that Paul had led Philemon to Christ. Because Paul was Philemon's spiritual father, he was hoping that Philemon would feel a debt of gratitude that he would repay by accepting Onesimus with a spirit of forgiveness.

1:22 Paul was released from prison soon after writing this letter, but the Bible doesn't say whether or not he returned to Colosse.

1:23 Epaphras was well known to the Colossians because he had founded the church there (Colossians 1:7). He was a hero to this church, helping to hold it together in spite of growing persecution and struggles with false doctrine. His report to Paul about the problems in Colosse had prompted Paul to write his letter to the Colossians. Epaphras's greetings to the Colossian Christians reveal his deep love for them (Colossians 4:12, 13). He may have been in prison with Paul for preaching the Good News.

1:24 Mark, Aristarchus, Demas, and Luke are also mentioned in Colossians 4:10, 14. Mark had accompanied Paul and Barnabas on their first missionary journey (Acts 12:25ff). Mark also wrote the Gospel of Mark. Luke had accompanied Paul on his third missionary journey and was the writer of the Gospel of Luke and the book of Acts. Demas had been faithful to Paul for a while but later deserted him (see 2 Timothy 4:10).

- **1:25** Paul urged Philemon to be reconciled to his slave, receiving him as a brother and fellow member of God's family. *Reconciliation* means reestablishing relationship. Christ has reconciled us to God and to others. Many barriers come between people—race, social status, sex, personality differences—but Christ can break down these barriers. Jesus Christ changed Onesimus's relationship to Philemon from slave to brother. Christ can transform our most hopeless relationships into deep and loving friendships.

STUDY QUESTIONS

Thirteen lessons for individual or group study

HOW TO USE THIS BIBLE STUDY

It's always exciting to get more than you expect. And that's what you'll find in this Bible study guide—much more than you expect. Our goal was to write thoughtful, practical, dependable, and application-oriented studies of God's word.

This study guide contains the complete text of the selected Bible book. The commentary is accurate, complete, and loaded with unique charts, maps, and profiles of Bible people.

With the Bible text, extensive notes and features, and questions to guide discussion, *Life Application Bible Studies* have everything you need in one place.

The lessons in this Bible study guide will work for large classes as well as small-group studies. To get everyone involved in your discussions, encourage participants to answer the questions before each meeting.

Each lesson is divided into five easy-to-lead sections. The section called "Reflect" introduces you and the members of your group to a specific area of life touched by the lesson. "Read" shows which chapters to read and which notes and other features to use. Additional questions help you understand the passage. "Realize" brings into focus the biblical principle to be learned with questions, a special insight, or both. "Respond" helps you make connections with your own situation and personal needs. The questions are designed to help you find areas in your life where you can apply the biblical truths. "Resolve" helps you map out action plans for that day.

Begin and end each lesson with prayer, asking for the Holy Spirit's guidance, direction, and wisdom.

Recommended time allotments for each section of a lesson are as follows:

Segment	60 minutes	90 minutes
Reflect on your life	*5 minutes*	*10 minutes*
Read the passage	*10 minutes*	*15 minutes*
Realize the principle	*15 minutes*	*20 minutes*
Respond to the message	*20 minutes*	*30 minutes*
Resolve to take action	*10 minutes*	*15 minutes*

All five sections work together to help a person learn the lessons, live out the principles, and obey the commands taught in the Bible.

Also, at the end of each lesson, there is a section entitled "More for studying other themes in this section." These questions will help you lead the group in studying other parts of each section not covered in depth by the main lesson.

But don't just listen to God's word. You must do what it says. Otherwise, you are only fooling yourselves. For if you listen to the word and don't obey, it is like glancing at your face in a mirror. You see yourself, walk away, and forget what you look like. But if you look carefully into the perfect law that sets you free, and if you do what it says and don't forget what you heard, then God will bless you for doing it. (James 1:22-25)

LESSON 1
HOW'S YOUR FOLLOW-THROUGH?
1 THESSALONIANS INTRODUCTION

REFLECT
on your life

1 When you buy a household appliance, what kind of service or support do you expect from the dealer after the sale?

_____

_____

_____

_____

_____

2 What do you appreciate about this support?

_____

_____

_____

_____

_____

READ
the passage

Read the introductory material to 1 Thessalonians, 1 Thessalonians 1:1, and the following note:

❐ 1:1

3 Given what we know about the city of Thessalonica, what problems might new Christians have had there?

_____

_____

_____

_____

4 What methods did Paul use to help the new Christians in Thessalonica get established in their faith?

_____

_____

_____

_____

5 What did Paul offer Thessalonica's new believers?

_____

_____

_____

_____

6 Why did Paul take responsibility for these new believers?

_____

_____

_____

Because Paul had to leave Thessalonica suddenly, he had no opportunity to fully instruct the new Christians there. But he did assume responsibility for them, first sending Timothy to them and then writing to them twice. New Christians need instruction from those who are older. This letter reminds us that we can have an ongoing influence on those who come to Christ.

REALIZE
the principle

7 What kinds of support do new Christians need?

_____

_____

_____

_____

8 What kinds of help or support can older Christians offer?

_____

_____

_____

_____

9 What can mature Christians do to encourage new believers?

_____

_____

_____

_____

10 How have you been able to help a new believer in the past?

_____

_____

_____

_____

_____

11 What does your church or group do to help new Christians grow in their faith?

_____

_____

_____

_____

_____

12 What else might your church or group do to help or support new Christians?

_____

_____

_____

_____

_____

13 Who are some of the newest believers in your church or among your circle of friends?

_____

_____

_____

_____

14 What could you do or say to encourage a new Christian within the next seven days?

RESOLVE
to take action

_____

_____

_____

_____

_____

A What is the best way to protect new Christians from misconceptions about Christ's return? about biblical doctrine in general? How can you be sure that *you* don't have misconceptions about Christ?

MORE
for studying
other themes
in this section

B What kind of reception did Paul and his associates get from the general population in Thessalonica (read Acts 17:1-9)? How did your non-Christian friends and acquaintances respond to you when they learned about your faith in Christ? What can you do to resolve or lessen the conflicts? What *can't* you do?

LESSON 2
COMING SOON!
1 THESSALONIANS 1:2-10

REFLECT
on your life

1 What is one thing you look forward to every day?

_____

_____

_____

_____

2 What do you look forward to in . . .

sports? _____

_____

family life? _____

_____

your line of work? _____

_____

your church? _____

_____

READ
the passage

Read 1 Thessalonians 1:2-10 and the following notes:

❏ 1:3   ❏ 1:6   ❏ 1:9, 10   ❏ 1:10

3 What were the Thessalonian believers anticipating (1:3)?

_____

_____

_____

4 What did these new Christians face because of their faith (1:6)?

_____

_____

_____

5 What happened as a result of their obedience to the Lord (1:7-9)?

_____

_____

_____

6 What does it take (mentally, emotionally, spiritually) to maintain a sense of continual anticipation?

_____

_____

_____

Three things about the Thessalonian believers impressed Paul. One of those things was their "enduring hope" of, or longing for, Christ's return. Perhaps their enthusiasm for this event can be attributed to their belief that Christ would return within their lifetime. The "severe suffering" they endured for their faith could also have provided the fuel they needed to long for Christ's return continually. But maybe their longing was similar to Paul's. That is, they just wanted to be in the presence of their Lord and Savior (see Philippians 1:23). Regardless of the reason for their anticipation, the Thessalonian believers set a good example for all Christians to follow. If we claim to be followers of Christ, we should long for his return. Are you eagerly looking forward to that day?

REALIZE
the principle

7 How do modern-day Christians compare with the Thessalonian believers in regard to anticipating Christ's return?

_____

_____

_____

8 What keeps some Christians from looking forward to Christ's return?

_____

_____

_____

9 What helps Christians look forward to and wait expectantly for Christ's return?

_____

_____

_____

RESPOND
to the message

10 What dulls your desire for Christ's return?

_____

_____

_____

11 How did this distraction gain a foothold in your life?

_____

_____

_____

12 What activities or relationships keep you from longing for Christ's return?

_____

_____

_____

RESOLVE
to take action

13 What activity, desire, or relationship do you need to give up in order to recapture an eager anticipation of meeting Christ one day?

_____

_____

_____

_____

14 What do you need to begin doing this week to strengthen your desire for his return?

_____

_____

_____

_____

A How did Paul know that God had chosen the Thessalonians (1:4-5)? What evidence of God's work do you see in your life?

MORE
for studying
other themes
in this section

B Whom did the Thessalonians imitate (1:6)? How have older, more mature Christians served as examples for you? How can you be a good example?

C What did the Holy Spirit do for the Thessalonian believers that made them willing to undergo suffering and persecution (1:6)? How can you rely on the Holy Spirit in times of difficulty?

D The Thessalonian Christians changed so radically that many people noticed. Who would notice if you suddenly changed the way you live? What changes is God prompting you to make now?

LESSON 3
NO OFFENSE
1 THESSALONIANS 2:1-16

REFLECT
on your life

1 What is the most offensive sales pitch that you have ever heard?

_____

_____

_____

_____

2 What was offensive about it?

_____

_____

_____

_____

READ
the passage

Read 1 Thessalonians 2:1-16 and the following notes:

❑ 2:1, 2   ❑ 2:4-8   ❑ 2:9   ❑ 2:13   ❑ 2:14   ❑ 2:15, 16

3 What made people in Thessalonica angry (2:14-16)?

_____

_____

_____

4 How did Paul go out of his way to avoid offending people (2:3-12)?

_____

_____

_____

5 What kept Paul's enemies energized in opposing him (2:15-16)?

_____

_____

_____

Many people in Thessalonica did not like the gospel message. They were offended by it. They did what they could to discredit Paul—insulting, rejecting, and physically abusing the believers. So Paul did what he could to remain blameless—supporting himself financially, speaking gently, never using flattery. But he never altered the message itself. Many people are offended by the gospel. We can alter our method of delivery or the way we communicate so that we don't offend, but we must never alter the message itself.

REALIZE
the principle

6 How or why might the gospel be offensive to people?

_____

_____

_____

7 How do Christians sometimes change the message of Christ to make it less offensive?

_____

_____

_____

_____

8 What aspects of sharing the gospel turn off unbelievers?

_____

_____

_____

_____

9 What can a Christian do to avoid these turnoffs without compromising the gospel message?

_____

_____

_____

10 Why do you think people are offended by the gospel?

_____

_____

_____

11 Whom would you like to tell about Christ within the next year?

_____

_____

_____

12 What might be this person's objections to the gospel?

_____

_____

_____

_____

13 How could you answer those objections?

_____

_____

_____

14 What can you do to communicate the gospel better without watering it down?

_____

_____

_____

_____

15 With whom would you like to share your faith but haven't because of your fear that they might be offended by the message?

_____

_____

_____

_____

16 How can you prepare yourself to handle any objections these people may have to the gospel?

_____

_____

_____

_____

_____

MORE
for studying
other themes
in this section

A What price did Paul pay for sharing the gospel (2:2)? How do you react when following Christ causes you some sort of rejection or misunderstanding? What price might you have to pay to bring the message of Christ to others?

B How did the Thessalonians know that Paul and Silas were sincere (2:2-3)? How do people judge the sincerity of your convictions?

C How or why did Paul's hard work in Thessalonica help his witness (2:9)? In what situations can your work help your witness?

LESSON 4
STANDING ALONE
1 THESSALONIANS 2:17–3:13

REFLECT
on your life

1 Who taught you how to drive?

_____

_____

_____

2 When did you stop depending on that person's help?

_____

_____

_____

_____

READ
the passage

Read 1 Thessalonians 2:17–3:13 and the following notes:

❒ 2:18   ❒ 3:1-3   ❒ 3:4   ❒ 3:5   ❒ 3:7, 8

3 How did the Thessalonians have to stand alone (2:17-18)?

_____

_____

_____

_____

4 What did Paul fear would happen to the Thessalonians after he left (3:1-3, 5)?

_____

_____

_____

_____

5 How did the Thessalonians respond to this time of testing (3:6-10)?

_____

_____

_____

_____

Paul and his companions were forced to leave Thessalonica sooner than they wanted to, having been driven out by persecution. The new believers they left behind were hardly established in the faith. Yet without the support, teaching, or encouragement of older Christians, and despite the opposition they faced, they remained faithful to Christ. By the time Paul sent Timothy to find out how they were doing, they had become rooted in their faith. Because their faith rested in Christ himself, not in Paul, Timothy, or Silas, they passed the test. Pastors, church leaders, authors, and older Christians help us grow, but we must not become overly dependent on them. Eventually we need to stand alone in our faith. Then, when we are tested, as the Thessalonians were, our faith will survive.

REALIZE
the principle

6 How can a Christian become overly dependent on a leader, teacher, or mentor?

_____

_____

_____

_____

7 Why is it a problem for a Christian to require the presence or teaching of a particular person in order to grow?

_____

_____

_____

_____

8 When might a Christian's faith in Christ alone be tested?

_____

_____

_____

_____

_____

9 Who are your spiritual mentors?

RESPOND
to the message

_____

_____

_____

_____

_____

10 How have your mentors helped establish you in your faith?

_____

_____

_____

_____

_____

11 What kinds of situations could test what you've been taught?

_____

_____

_____

_____

12 What can you do to get ready for future challenges to your faith?

_____

_____

_____

_____

13 How could you say thank you to your spiritual mentors?

RESOLVE
to take action

_____

_____

_____

_____

14 What can you do to reaffirm your faith and trust in God alone this week?

_____

_____

_____

_____

_____

A Because Paul could not go to Thessalonica, he sent Timothy in his place (3:2). What made Timothy qualified to go? What skills could you learn that would enable you to minister to others more?

B In what ways can Satan hinder your service to God (2:18; 3:5)? What else hinders your service to God? What can you do to remove or cope with these obstacles?

C What satanic activity did Paul fear would take place against the church at Thessalonica (3:5)? What can you do to be prepared for Satan's schemes?

D How did the Thessalonians encourage Paul (3:8)?

E What risks did Paul take because he loved the Thessalonians? What risks have you had to take for the people you love? What risks might you have to take in the future?

MORE
for studying
other themes
in this section

LESSON 5
JUST LIKE THE GOOD OLD DAYS
1 THESSALONIANS 4:1-12

REFLECT
on your life

1 What evidence do you see of low moral standards in today's society?

_____

_____

_____

_____

2 How have these low standards affected you?

_____

_____

_____

_____

READ
the passage

Read 1 Thessalonians 4:1-12 and the following notes:

❏ 4:1-8   ❏ 4:3

3 What is God's will for us (4:3)?

_____

_____

_____

4 What does it mean to live holy lives (4:3-7)?

_____

_____

_____

_____

5 Why is it important for us to be holy (4:6-8)?

_____

_____

_____

_____

_____

6 What bearing does self-control have on living a holy life?

_____

_____

_____

_____

_____

In this section of his letter, Paul taught the Christians at Thessalonica how to avoid sexual immorality. The temptations they faced were real, and the peer pressure around them could not be ignored. So Paul reminded them that God had called them to holiness. Sexual sins can destroy marriages, ruin reputations, and remove Christians from opportunities to minister. Worst of all, sexual sins break our fellowship with God and invite his punishment. The need to maintain control over our own body, especially in an immoral society, is crucial.

REALIZE
the principle

7 Why is it important for a Christian to be self-controlled?

_____

_____

_____

_____

_____

8 What makes it difficult for any person to control his or her body (4:3-5)?

_____

_____

_____

_____

_____

9 When is a person most vulnerable to losing control sexually?

RESPOND
to the message

_____

_____

_____

_____

_____

_____

10 How can a person become less vulnerable to sexual immorality?

_____

_____

_____

_____

_____

_____

11 What resources can a Christian depend on to help him or her stay pure?

_____

_____

_____

_____

_____

_____

12 What can you do this week to strengthen your resolve to stay pure?

RESOLVE
to take action

_____

_____

_____

_____

_____

_____

A What instructions and warnings did Paul remind the Thessalonians about (4:1-12)? How can you remember God's instructions to you?

B What were the Thessalonians instructed to do to win the respect of unbelievers (4:11-12)? What actions enable Christians today to win the respect of unbelievers? How might you be more sensitive to this part of your witness?

MORE
for studying
other themes
in this section

LESSON 6
GET READY, GET SET . . .
1 THESSALONIANS 4:13–5:11

REFLECT
on your life

1 How did you prepare for this lesson or series of lessons?

_____

_____

_____

_____

2 How do you get ready for a vacation?

_____

_____

_____

_____

_____

READ
the passage

Read 1 Thessalonians 4:13–5:11, the chart "The Events of Christ's Return" (found near 1 Thessalonians 2), and the following notes:

❒ 4:13ff   ❒ 5:1-3   ❒ 5:2

3 Why did the Thessalonians want to know when Christ would return (4:13-18)?

_____

_____

_____

_____

4 When will Christ return (5:1-3)?

_____

_____

_____

5 How can Christians get ready for Christ's return (5:6-11)?

_____

_____

_____

The Thessalonian Christians were anxious for Christ's return. They thought that Christ was going to come back while they were all still alive. They also thought that those who had already died would not rise from the dead. When some of them did die and Christ had not returned, they became confused and anxious. Paul reassured them that *all* Christians who die will rise from their graves. And he stressed that no one knows "when all this will happen" (5:1). The time of Christ's second coming will surprise everyone, so we should take pains to be ready. Christians of nearly every generation have speculated about when Christ will come again. But none of us know *when*. We know only that he will return. What matters is that we be ready for Christ at any moment.

REALIZE
the principle

6 How or why do arguments about the time of Christ's coming distract us from getting ready?

_____

_____

_____

7 Why do some Christians believe others' speculations about the exact timing of Christ's return?

_____

_____

_____

8 What is the best response to predictions about Christ's return?

_____

_____

_____

_____

9 How can Christians help unbelievers get ready for Christ's return?

_____

_____

_____

_____

RESPOND
to the message

10 Knowing that Christ will return someday, how can you use your time and resources more wisely?

_____

_____

_____

_____

11 What can you do to be ready for Christ to return?

_____

_____

_____

_____

12 How can Christians encourage one another with the certainty of Christ's second coming?

_____

_____

_____

_____

RESOLVE
take action

13 What changes in yourself—your habits, lifestyle, or prayer life—would make you more ready for Christ's return than you are now?

_____

_____

_____

_____

A Why were the Thessalonian Christians worried about their dead loved ones (4:13-18)? How did Paul encourage them? Whom can you encourage with this news?

MORE
for studying
other themes
in this section

B Why will unbelievers be surprised when Christ returns (5:2)? Why will Christians be able to respond differently (5:4)? How can you share your hope in Christ with your friends?

C How would you paraphrase the command "Stay alert and be clearheaded" (5:6)? In what contexts is it important for a Christian to be alert and clear-headed? In what areas of your life do you exhibit these qualities, and in what areas do you need to develop them?

LESSON 7
THE LAST WORD
1 THESSALONIANS 5:12-28

R
REFLECT
n your life

1 What are some famous last words you have heard or read?

_____

_____

_____

_____

2 What final piece of advice would you give a son or daughter about to leave for college?

_____

_____

_____

_____

R
EAD
e passage

Read 1 Thessalonians 5:12-28 and the following notes:

❐ 5:14   ❐ 5:17   ❐ 5:18   ❐ 5:19   ❐ 5:28

3 What are a Christian's responsibilities toward leaders (5:12-13)?

_____

_____

_____

4 What should Christians do for one another (5:14-15)?

_____

_____

_____

5 What were Paul's final instructions about a Christian's relationship with God (5:16-22)?

_____

_____

_____

In these closing words, Paul summarized much of what he had been teaching the Thessalonian Christians. With instructions about their relationships with leaders, with one another, and with God, he gave a balanced view of what the Christian life should be. If believers fail in any of these relationships, it soon shows up in other areas. By dishonoring the people God places in our life, we dishonor God.

REALIZE
the principle

6 How do some Christians honor their church leaders?

_____

_____

7 In 5:14, what does it mean to . . .

"warn those who are lazy"? _____

_____

"encourage those who are timid"? _____

_____

"take tender care of those who are weak"?_____

_____

"be patient with everyone"? _____

_____

8 How do people retaliate?

_____

_____

_____

9 What is the difference between joy and happiness?

_____

_____

_____

10 What is a prayerful attitude?

_____

_____

_____

_____

11 How can a Christian always be thankful "in all circumstances" (5:18)?

_____

_____

_____

_____

12 How might a person "stifle the Holy Spirit" (5:19)?

_____

_____

_____

_____

RESPOND
the message

13 Which acts of obedience do you consider most difficult?

_____

_____

_____

_____

_____

14 What steps could you take to overcome those difficulties and be more obedient?

_____

_____

_____

_____

_____

_____

15 Which of the steps listed above will you take this week?

_____

_____

_____

_____

RESOLVE
to take action

16 When will you do it?

_____

_____

_____

_____

A What are some practical ways you can "stay away from every kind of evil" (5:22)? How can you do this but remain involved in the lives of unbelievers in your neighborhood, community, and extended family?

B What does it mean for God to make someone "holy in every way" (5:23)? How do you resist God's work in your life? Which area(s) of your life do you tend to keep from God? What change(s) would make you more consistent?

MORE
for studying
other themes
in this section

LESSON 8
YOU CAN SAY THAT AGAIN!
2 THESSALONIANS INTRODUCTION

REFLECT
on your life

1 What do you think the statement "I'll meet you there at half past" means?

_____

_____

_____

_____

2 How could the above statement be misunderstood?

_____

_____

_____

_____

3 Why do people sometimes misunderstand clear messages?

_____

_____

_____

_____

READ
the passage

Read the introductory material to 2 Thessalonians and the following note:

❐ 1:1

4 What message did the Thessalonians have trouble understanding correctly?

_____

_____

_____

5 What problems were created by this misunderstanding?

_____

_____

_____

6 How did persecution complicate the situation?

_____

_____

_____

7 How did Paul help them clear up the misunderstanding and the problems created by it?

_____

_____

_____

The Thessalonian Christians were like most of us—subject to misunderstanding the word of God. When Paul taught them about the return of Christ, many of them misunderstood. As a result, they misinterpreted and misapplied what he had told them. Paul had to write again to clear up their confusion and head off the errors being created by it—especially laziness and fear. It is perfectly human to misunderstand a message. Sometimes we may misunderstand the Bible, read into it what we want it to say, or use a passage out of context to support our opinion. That is why we, like the Thessalonians, need help understanding the message God has for us.

REALIZE
the principle

8 Why do people misunderstand the Bible?

_____

_____

_____

_____

9 What provision has God made for us to understand his message to us?

_____

_____

_____

_____

10 Where can a Christian turn when confused about what God wants?

_____

_____

_____

_____

_____

R
ESPOND
the message

11 What passages from the Bible have you found confusing or difficult to under-stand, either now or at some time in the past?

_____

_____

_____

12 What have you done to find answers to your questions about the Bible?

_____

_____

_____

_____

_____

13 Who might be able to help you understand biblical passages?

_____

_____

_____

_____

_____

R
ESOLVE
take action

14 What passage or idea in Scripture is still difficult for you to understand?

_____

_____

_____

_____

15 What will you do this week to gain a better understanding of this passage or idea?

_____

_____

_____

_____

A How can we strike a proper balance between serving Christ daily and waiting expectantly for his return?

B How can we keep our Christian friends mindful of the fact that Christ could return soon?

C If Christ were to come within the next three hours, what would you need to do to be ready?

MORE
for studying
other themes
in this section

LESSON 9
OUT IN THE COLD
2 THESSALONIANS 1:1-12

REFLECT
on your life

1 If you were shopping for the following items, what defects would make you reject them?

A piece of fruit: _____

_____

A house: _____

_____

Clothes: _____

_____

2 For what reasons do some people reject others?

_____

_____

_____

_____

_____

READ
the passage

Read 2 Thessalonians 1:1-12 and the following notes:

❐ 1:1 ❐ 1:4 ❐ 1:4-6 ❐ 1:5 ❐ 1:7

3 How is our society like the Thessalonian society?

_____

_____

_____

_____

4 What were the Christians living in Thessalonica experiencing (1:4-6)?

_____

_____

_____

_____

5 How did Paul encourage them (1:5-10)?

_____

_____

_____

_____

_____

Much of what Paul wrote to the Thessalonians dealt directly with persecution. Because they believed in Christ, they were persecuted by friends, misunderstood by acquaintances, and scorned by work associates. Paul encouraged them to continue to trust God. In the end, God would reward those who believed in him and punish those who rejected and attacked his followers. It is easy to get discouraged when people reject or turn cold toward you because they have rejected God, his word, his people, or his ways. At times, the pain of rejection can be acute. But when you trust God, he gives you the grace to continue.

REALIZE
the principle

6 What similarities do you see between your circumstances and those of the Thessalonian believers?

_____

_____

_____

_____

7 How can Christians and churches benefit from persecution?

_____

_____

_____

_____

_____

8 What do believers need to remember most when they are persecuted for their faith?

_____

_____

_____

_____

_____

9 What are you tempted to do when you are persecuted (regardless of what you are persecuted for)?

_____

_____

_____

_____

10 In what situations or at what times might you be persecuted for your faith in Christ?

_____

_____

_____

_____

11 What will help you keep your focus on Christ when you respond to persecution?

_____

_____

_____

_____

12 When your faith or values clash with those of others, what might you say or do in response to glorify God and be respectful to others?

_____

_____

_____

_____

_____

13 In what situations over the next few days might you be persecuted for your faith?

_____

_____

_____

_____

RESOLVE
to take action

14 What will help you be prepared?

_____

_____

_____

_____

A What made Paul thankful for the Thessalonians (1:3-4)? What can you do to become a person for whom others thank God?

B When will God give his people relief from persecution (1:6-7)? How can God use suffering and persecution in your life?

C When Christ returns, what will happen to those who don't know him (1:6-10)? What can you do to help change the heart of an unbeliever you know?

MORE
for studying
other themes
in this section

LESSON 10
JUST CHECKING
2 THESSALONIANS 2:1-17

REFLECT
n your life

1 How do you verify . . .

a telephone number?_____

_____

_____

a quotation?_____

_____

_____

a destination? _____

_____

_____

historical facts?_____

_____

_____

2 Why might it be important to verify something?

_____

_____

_____

_____

EAD
e passage

Read 2 Thessalonians 2:1-17 and the following notes:

❐ 2:2   ❐ 2:3ff   ❐ 2:10-12   ❐ 2:15

3 What is the "day of the Lord" (2:1-2)?

_____

_____

_____

4 Why did some Thessalonian Christians think that the day of the Lord had already begun (2:2)?

_____

_____

_____

_____

5 How could they have avoided being fooled (2:3, 5, 15)?

_____

_____

_____

One snare that all Christians must avoid is deceivers. In Thessalonica certain people were saying (wrongly) that the day of the Lord had already begun. And many Christians believed them. "Don't be fooled by what they say," Paul told them (2:3), explaining how the day of the Lord would come about. Many people have claimed to speak for God. Because false prophets or teachers often sound convincing, even Christians can be fooled. We can avoid being led astray by measuring what a teacher says by the word of God (2:15).

REALIZE
the principle

6 Why is it important to hold fast to the truth about God and what he wants?

_____

_____

_____

_____

7 What has God given his people to keep them from being fooled?

_____

_____

_____

_____

8 What makes people vulnerable to deception?

RESPOND
the message

_____

_____

_____

_____

_____

9 To what kinds of deception are Christians vulnerable?

_____

_____

_____

_____

10 What steps can a Christian take to keep from being fooled?

_____

_____

_____

_____

11 What could you do to understand God's word better?

_____

_____

_____

_____

_____

12 For whom might you pray that God will keep him or her from being fooled by false teaching?

RESOLVE
take action

_____

_____

_____

_____

_____

13 This week pray that God will point out errors in your thinking, beliefs, lifestyle, or actions.

A What does it mean that "this lawlessness is already at work secretly" (2:7)? In what ways was it at work when Paul wrote? In what ways is it at work today?

MORE
for studying
other themes
in this section

B Why does God cause some people "to be greatly deceived" so that "they will believe these lies" (2:11)? How can you guard against this?

C God saves us by grace (2:16). How or why are we undeserving of God's special favor? What are some reasonable responses to God's special favor?

LESSON 11
IDLE WORSHIP
2 THESSALONIANS 3:1-18

1 Laziness is . . .

_____

_____

_____

_____

2 Without mentioning names, describe the laziest person you have ever worked with.

_____

_____

_____

_____

_____

Read 2 Thessalonians 3:1-18 and the following notes:

❐ 3:6-10   ❐ 3:6-15   ❐ 3:14, 15

3 Who was shirking responsibility in Thessalonica (3:6)?

_____

_____

4 What should they have been doing instead (3:7-10)?

_____

_____

_____

5 What was the cure for their laziness (3:11-15)?

_____

_____

_____

_____

The Christians at Thessalonica were using the return of Christ as an excuse to be lazy. Believing that Christ would come back any day, they quit their jobs and waited. Paul wrote and told them to get back to work. Even if Christ were about to return, they were not absolved of their responsibilities. God wants us to fulfill all of the responsibilities he has given us while we wait for Christ to return. That is the way we carry out his will.

REALIZE
the principle

6 What responsibilities has God given every Christian?

_____

_____

_____

7 What causes people to shirk their responsibilities?

_____

_____

_____

_____

8 What excuses do people use to justify laziness?

_____

_____

_____

_____

9 When is it best to "warn those who are lazy" (1 Thessalonians 5:14)?

_____

_____

_____

_____

10 When is it best to "stay away from all believers who live idle lives" (2 Thessalonians 3:6)?

_____

_____

_____

_____

_____

11 What responsibilities has God given you?

RESPOND
the message

_____

_____

_____

_____

_____

12 When are you tempted to shirk your responsibilities?

_____

_____

_____

_____

13 What will it mean for you to be diligent and not lazy?

_____

_____

_____

_____

_____

14 How can you improve the way you use your time at work?

_____

_____

_____

_____

15 What is satisfactory about the way you now use your free time?

_____

_____

_____

16 What adjustments do you need to make in the way you use rest or relaxation time?

_____

_____

_____

_____

17 How can you alter the use of your time this week to better reflect your responsibilities?

_____

_____

_____

_____

_____

RESOLVE
to take action

A Paul asked the Thessalonians to pray that he would be delivered from evil people (3:2). Why is it important to ask for prayer? What prayer requests do you need to share with others? Whose requests will you pray for this week?

B Paul exhorted the Thessalonians to never tire of doing good (3:13). What did Paul mean by this? Do you ever tire of doing good? If so, why? How can you continue to do good even when you don't want to or are tired of it?

MORE
for studying
other themes
in this section

LESSON 12
SUPER SERVICE
PHILEMON 1:1-7

1 How would you describe excellent service . . .

from a gas station?_____

_____

_____

in a grocery store? _____

_____

_____

from a mail-order company? _____

_____

_____

at a church? _____

_____

_____

2 Who or what makes the difference at these places?

_____

_____

_____

_____

_____

_____

Read the introductory material to Philemon, Philemon 1:1-7, and the following notes:

❒ 1:1   ❒ 1:2   ❒ 1:4-7

3 Why did Paul thank God for Philemon (1:4-5)?

_____

_____

_____

_____

4 How did Philemon, who was not a pastor, serve and minister to people in the church (1:4-7)?

_____

_____

_____

_____

_____

We know from what Paul wrote that Philemon was not a pastor or a paid church-staff member but just a Christian living in Colosse. Yet rather than merely attending church, Philemon opened his home to other Christians so they could meet together. And, as Paul says with praise, Philemon loved God's people. You do not have to hold a formal position in the church to serve God. God uses many people to accomplish his work. Some of them are formal leaders of local churches. Many others are simply Christians who have opened their homes and shown their love for believers in tangible ways.

REALIZE
the principle

5 Why is it important for all Christians—not just formal leaders—to minister?

_____

_____

_____

_____

_____

6 In your church, what holds people back from serving?

_____

_____

_____

_____

RESPOND
to the message

7 How can Christians be motivated to serve more?

_____

_____

_____

_____

8 What are some of the ways you now serve in your church?

_____

_____

_____

_____

9 How might you open your home for ministry?

_____

_____

_____

_____

_____

10 How else can you serve God's people?

_____

_____

_____

_____

_____

11 What act of service could you perform in the next week or two?

ESOLVE
take action

_____

_____

_____

_____

_____

A How did Philemon use his wealth to serve God (1:1-2)? What resources do you have to serve God? Whom could you help with these resources?

B What effect did Philemon's life have on others (1:4-7)? What effect does your life have on others? What could you do to be more conscious of your example to others?

MORE
for studying
other themes
in this section

LESSON 13
TEARING DOWN BARRIERS
PHILEMON 1:8-25

REFLECT
on your life

1 What kind of barrier would you put up if you wanted to . . .

keep your house warm in the winter?_____

_____

_____

divert floodwaters?_____

_____

_____

separate fighting siblings? _____

_____

_____

2 What sort of barriers do people put up between each other?

_____

_____

_____

READ
the passage

Read Philemon 1:8-25 and the following notes:

❏ 1:10ff ❏ 1:11-15 ❏ 1:16 ❏ 1:19 ❏ 1:25

3 Onesimus had run away but later agreed to go back to slavery. What happened to bring about this change (1:10)?

_____

_____

_____

_____

4 What assurance did Paul have that Philemon would take Onesimus back (1:19-21)?

_____

_____

_____

_____

5 Paul, Onesimus, and Philemon each made a sacrifice of some kind. What was each one's difficult decision?

Paul: _____

_____

_____

_____

Onesimus: _____

_____

_____

_____

Philemon: _____

_____

_____

_____

6 Who do you think paid the biggest price?

_____

_____

_____

_____

Philemon had every reason to be harsh with Onesimus. In fact, according to Roman law at that time, he could have had Onesimus killed for running away. And very few people would have faulted him for it. But God's love—accepted by Philemon first and later by Onesimus—simply took away those reasons. Christ breaks down the barriers we build between each other. Race, ethnicity, gender, social status, and many other human factors divide ordinary people. Love for Christ moves us to tear down the barriers that can otherwise cause so much grief.

REALIZE
the principle

7 What is the basis for tearing down the barriers that the world uses to divide people?

_____

_____

_____

_____

_____

8 What barriers divide many people today?

ESPOND
• the message

_____

_____

_____

_____

_____

9 What can we learn about tearing down barriers . . .

from Paul? _____

_____

_____

from Onesimus? _____

_____

_____

from Philemon? _____

_____

_____

10 With what person or people can you tear down a barrier?

_____

_____

_____

_____

_____

11 What can you do or say this week to break down barriers between yourself
and others?

RESOLVE
to take action

_____

_____

_____

_____

_____

_____

A In what ways is the letter to Philemon a model for employer-employee
relationships? How might you modify your actions toward your employer in
obedience to Christ?

MORE
for studying
other themes
in this section

B Paul used tact in this letter to Philemon. What can we learn from Paul about
approaching people with whom we have a difficult or unpleasant matter to
discuss? In what situations do you need tact? How can you use honest praise
or affirmation to help in these situations?

C Paul was taking some risks by appealing to Philemon. What risks do we
take when we try to help people resolve their differences? What practical
steps can a mediator take to lessen the risk?

Take Your Bible Study
to the Next Level

The *Life Application Study Bible* helps you apply truths in God's Word to everyday life. It's packed with nearly 10,000 notes and features that make it today's #1–selling study Bible.

Life Application Notes: Thousands of Life Application notes help explain God's Word and challenge you to apply the truth of Scripture to your life.

Personality Profiles: You can benefit from the life experiences of over a hundred Bible figures.

Book Introductions: These provide vital statistics, an overview, and a timeline to help you quickly understand the message of each book.

Maps: Over 200 maps next to the Bible text highlight important Bible places and events.

Christian Worker's Resource: Enhance your ministry effectiveness with this practical supplement.

Charts: Over 260 charts help explain difficult concepts and relationships.

Harmony of the Gospels: Using a unique numbering system, the events from all four Gospels are harmonized into one chronological account.

Daily Reading Plan: This reading plan is your guide to reading through the entire Bible in one unforgettable year.

Topical Index: A master index provides instant access to Bible passages and features that address the topics on your mind.

Dictionary/Concordance: With entries for many of the important words in the Bible, this is an excellent starting place for studying the Bible text.

Available in the New Living Translation, New International Version, King James Version, and New King James Version. Take an interactive tour of the *Life Application Study Bible* at
www.NewLivingTranslation.com/LASB

CP0271